UNDER THE SUN

UNDER THE SUN

IMPRESSIONS OF INDIAN CITIES:

WITH A CHAPTER DEALING WITH

THE LATER LIFE OF NANA SAHIB

PERCEVAL LANDON

GYAN

Published by

GYAN

Gyan Publishing House
5, Ansari Road
Daryaganj, New Delhi-110002
Phone: 011-47034999, 9811692060
E-mail: books@gyanbooks.com

Distribution Network
gyanbooks.com
India, USA, Canada, UK, Australia, France

ISBN: 978-81-212-9118-7 (PB)
First Published, 1906

2nd Impression 2023

Printed at: Gyan Press, Delhi.

UNDER THE SUN
AUTHOR: PERCEVAL LANDON

UNDER THE SUN

THE TASHI LAMA AT BUDDHGAYA.

UNDER THE SUN

IMPRESSIONS OF INDIAN CITIES: WITH A CHAPTER DEALING WITH THE LATER LIFE OF NANA SAHIB

BY

PERCEVAL LANDON

AUTHOR OF "LHASA"

"In Ynde ben fulle manye dyverse Contrees."

—Sir John Maundevile.

LONDON

HURST AND BLACKETT, LTD.

1906

THE CHAPEL RIVER PRESS
KINGSTON SURREY

TO

SIR FRANK YOUNGHUSBAND

PREFACE.

UPON the title-page I have placed Sir John's comment, which to this day remains the beginning and the end of all Indian knowledge. These chapters have been written in the course of annual wanderings over India during the last five years, and their intention is to indicate—if the unhappy phrase must be used—the widely different local colour that distinguishes one Indian city from another. "Under the Sun" is not a record of the late tour of the Prince of Wales, nor is it in any sense a guide-book. But as a companion to that invaluable volume it may perhaps be of use to those who find a difficulty in making a picture out of the wealth of detailed Indian information which every traveller now possesses. There are also some tales.

The chapter dealing with the hitherto unknown later days of Nana Sahib may seem somewhat out of keeping with the rest of the book. I am, however, confident that, on the contrary, these will prove to no few the most interesting pages in the volume, and my excuse for inserting them here must be that their small compass—which I did not wish to expand by adding in any way to the bald historical facts that are here presented for the first time—made their separate publication somewhat difficult. I owe thanks to many both in India and at home, and especially I wish to acknowledge the kindness of the proprietors of the *Daily Telegraph*, in whose columns I was enabled to sum up in a series of letters a part of what is here recast in a more permanent form.

PERCEVAL LANDON.

5, Pall Mall Place, S.W.

CONTENTS.

	PAGE
PREFACE	vii
BOMBAY	1
AN INDIAN RAILWAY JOURNEY	12
UDAIPUR	26
JAIPUR	37
DELHI	49
LAHORE	59
THE KHYBER	69
AGRA	82
JAMMU	92
CALCUTTA	101
DARJILING	110
PURI	119
RANGOON	132
MANDALAY	144
MADRAS	154
COCHIN AND KOTTYAM	167
HYDERABAD	179
GWALIOR	190
CAWNPORE	198
AMRITSAR	209
BIKANIR	222
BENARES	232
BUDDH-GAYA	241
SOUTH INDIA	258
THE LATER DAYS OF NANA SAHIB	272

LIST OF ILLUSTRATIONS.

The Tashi Lama at Buddh-Gaya (*coloured*) . . *Frontispiece*
Malabar Point, Bombay . . . . . . *Facing page* 4
A Bhairagi . . . . „ „ 8
The Elephants' Bathing Pool (*photogravure*) . „ „ 16
Chitor . . . . „ „ 26
From the Palace: Udaipur . . . . . . „ „ 28
Jag Mandar . . . . „ „ 30
Udaipur (*photogravure*) . . . . . . „ „ 32
The Royal Palace, Udaipur . . . . . „ „ 34
On the Lake: Udaipur . . . . „ „ 36
Amber Palace . . . . „ „ 40
A Corner of the Diwan-i-Khas . . . . . „ „ 56
Ahmedabad (*photogravure*) . . . . . . „ „ 60
Kim on Zam-Zammah . . . . „ „ 62
The Shalimar Gardens, Lahore . . . . . „ „ 70
The End of the Grand Trunk Road, beyond Landi Kotal . . . . „ „ 70
A Kafila in the Khyber Pass . . . . . „ „ 80
The Taj (*photogravure*) . . . . „ „ 88
Jammu . . . . „ „ 96
Nadoun, Keeper of the Tigers, Jammu . . . „ „ 98
Sunrise on the Hugli (*coloured*) . . . . . . „ „ 102
A Calcutta Sunset (*photogravure*) . . . . „ „ 104
Sunset from the Fort, Calcutta (*coloured*) . . „ „ 108
The Temple of Jaganath, Puri (*photogravure*) . „ „ 120
The Temple of Jaganath, Puri . . . . . „ „ 128
A Burmese Monastery . . . . „ „ 132
A Corner in a Monastery Compound . . . . „ „ 136
The Shwé Dagôn . . . . „ „ 140
Chitor . . . . „ „ 144
Mandalay . . . . „ „ 144
The Queen's Golden Monastery, Mandalay (*photogravure*) . . . . „ „ 150

Mahabalipuram (*coloured*)	*Facing page*	160
Hampi (*photogravure*)	" "	164
Siva's Temple at the Seven Pagodas (*coloured*)	" "	166
Cochin Creek	" "	168
A Woman of Travancore	" "	170
The Synagogue of the White Jews, Cochin	" "	172
The Church, Kottyam	" "	172
Entrance to the Church, Kottyam	" "	176
Quilon (*coloured*)	" "	178
Aurangzeb's Tomb, Roza	" "	184
Golconda	" "	184
Srirangam (*photogravure*)	" "	192
The Treasury Square, Amritsar	" "	212
Sikh Devotees at Amritsar	" "	216
City Gate, Bikanir	" "	224
Gossips in Bikanir	" "	226
Drawing Water: Bikanir	" "	226
A Street in Bikanir	" "	230
The Burning Ghat, Benares (*photogravure*)	" "	232
The only Temple to Brahma in India, on the shores of Pushkar Lake	" "	236
The greatest Temple to Siva: the Golden Temple, Benares	" "	238
The largest Temple in India: view of Forbidden Sanctuary of Vishnu's Temple, Srirangam	" "	238
The Lion Pillar recently found at Sarnath, near Benares	" "	240
Buddh-Gaya	" "	244
Asoka's Railing, Buddh-Gaya	" "	244
The Great Buddha on the Diamond Throne, Buddh-Gaya	" "	250
Under the Bô-tree, Buddh-Gaya	" "	254
Buddh-Gaya (*coloured*)	" "	256
The Old Dutch Fort, Quilon	" "	258
The Main Gateway, Tanjore	" "	260
Buddhist Cave, Ellora (*photogravure*)	" "	262
A Sanctuary in Madura	" "	264
The Processional Car, Seringapatam	" "	266
In a South Indian Temple.	" "	266
Rameswaram (*photogravure*)	" "	268

UNDER THE SUN.

Bombay.

THE fifth morning out from Aden raises India from the sea ahead, a grey wraith of jagged mountain spurs along the horizon to the east. Flat and ash-purple against the dawn, touched still with the last skeins of the vapours of the starry night, the hills stand sentinel about Bombay island and that all-precious inner harbour which nestles between the spit on which the city lies and the rugged mainland beyond. The ranges seem but a low-lying confusion at the first, but as they strain themselves apart, Salsette and Matheran and Khandala—thrones of mystery not unfit to form the background of the entering-in of Asia—are to be distinguished long before the first sight of Bombay itself is possible. There is another hour's steaming before the uttermost point of Malabar Hill, with its solitary casuarina and its rock-perched bungalow, slides forward to the north-east, tipping with a flash of white the long recurving line of Back Bay. This is the real sea-front of the huge city, but it is sand-shallowed and useless for shipping. It stretches out unburdened, except for a few rude cock-boats showing where some pomphlet fishermen are engaged on their eternal search among the cork-dotted nets below the woods of Government House. Shallow, indeed, is Back Bay. The Governor cannot find water deep enough even for a steam launch from the Point to the Secretariat on the shore, but drives round daily under the trees, in scarlet state, four mounted sowars before and four behind. A moment later the eye can pick out the Rajabai clock tower, and soon the crowding domes, roofs, and pinnacles of Bombay detach themselves, one by one, from the neutral background across the harbour. But we are still far from our goal. For Bombay faces east, not west, and a steamer has to double the Prong lighthouse at the extremest tip of the island before she can swing up, northerly and deliberately, to an anchorage past the tiny little grass-grown fort of Oyster Rock. It is shoal water here, and we thrash up a tawny wash of mud through the full opaque green of the still harbour. At last the backing screws thrust forward the tumultuous discoloured flood to our very bows, and the anchor plunges with iron wrath into it, tearing behind it the clattering, rusty entrails of the bows, and the long journey is at an end. We can lean over the side and watch India as she lies out in the morning sun.

Bombay hangs like an Oriental ear-jewel across the sea-mouth of this bowl of bare hills filled with green water. She is, at very sea-level, ten miles in length from Siwa to the Prong; to the north she hangs from the forbidding mass of Salsette by four strands of rail and road, and—she is the Gate of India. Like other gates, she enjoys the privileges and dignities of portalhood—chiefly ostentation of architecture and a proper recognition of her own importance. Like other gates, she also pays the price that all straitened entries have to pay. For chiefly in the gate is the clash and jar of custom and caste, race and occupation, and the fierce jostling of the exchanging caravan and merchandise,—nay, for what other reason is ready justice administered in the town-gate but this, that here is the shoulder-rubbing that ever draws mankind like iron in the hand. There is no extinguisher of character like a turnstile, and no janitor but has his touch of Gallio. Let us hear the conclusion of the whole matter. Bombay has little or no individuality.

This is why so many a writer has tried to describe Bombay, and why so often the result is negative, though using half a lac of words. Simply, it cannot be done. She has no threads of continuity; she has no point of reference, no inner meaning. First and foremost, she stands for a practical need that comes home equally to all those who occupy their business along the west coast of India—and she stands for little else. It would be easy to tell some scrap of the tale of the moving panorama in the streets; it has been done, and well done, not once nor twice, nor thrice. Yet the glowing adjectives of a Chevrillon or a Steevens, or the quick and certain classification of an Arnold, will not, when all is said and done, give you more than one aspect of the great metropolis of the west. Jostling each other in the streets of the bazaar there are half the races of India. From hairy hill-men of the north-west, independent sons of Islam, wearing, despite their unkempt toilette, silk damasks and turquoise-studded belts of sambar-skin, bestitched and inlaid with colour, such as no other part of India can rival, to the six-sevenths

Malabar Point, Bombay.

[*Facing page* 4.

naked bhistie, with his soiled loin-cloth dividing into three his sweating, burnt-sienna skin, you will find an example of almost every one of the main divisions of the inhabitants of India. But, if you look, you will find that these men are all strangers like yourself. Like you, a transitory necessity drives them into the Empire's gate; but they have no home here, no abiding place, and, like you, as with a sigh you put on your sola topi once again, one and all are counting the days till they return homewards to plain, or coast, or mountain. All, that is, except the colourless and neutral residents of the bazaar, myriad hewers of wood and drawers of water to their vivid and attention-compelling guests, and except also the Parsees.

Bombay has been made by the Parsees as much as by ourselves. The Huguenots of the East, they have acquired power and wealth in the land of their exile; and their black-varnished scuttle hats, unbrimmed and ugly beyond even the top-hat of the West, are the fittest emblems of Bombay's unruffled commercial prosperity. The native name for them, "crows," is, in some ways, not unjust. They have reaped where others have sown. The merchant 'venturers of England cleared their way for them, and if they have now reached the uttermost flood of their fortune, their future is not so much in doubt from any slackening of their keen business traits as from the restraint of marriage that their stringent code enjoins.

The history of Bombay is half a romance, half a copy-book maxim.* They were shrewd men in the old days, who rented the dowry of the Infanta from Charles II. at £10 a year "for ever." Against the assaults of the Admiral of Janjira and the Dutch alike, these imperial gamblers clung stubbornly to their malarious spit of land between two waters, clung on through long and evil years, till their overbearing rival, Surat, was slowly silted up in the sands of the Tapti, and the impatient tide of commerce felt its way anew southward to its only other outlet. To-day their successors have reaped a reward indeed. Karachi is an overflow meeting rather than a rival attraction. Through Bombay the tides of men and merchandise must flow. But in its development Bombay has grown up in such manner as seaports must needs grow. Shanghai, Hong Kong, Singapore, Calcutta itself —all alike suffer this loss of identity beneath the

* At one time Cromwell was far-sighted enough to think of capturing Bombay. There is a rumour that when he communicated his idea to them, his ministers had some idea that Bombay was near Brazil.

cross-currents of commerce, that leveller of prejudice and pride. It were as inept to quote the Queen's Road as characteristic of Bombay as the bazaar or the wooded gardens and villas of Malabar Hill. Elphinstone Circle, though a trifle out of date, has its own separate story to tell, and the dockyard, the Yacht Club, Mazagoon, and Byculla each has its significance in this kaleidoscopic gallimaufry; only the caves of Elephanta seem meaningless and forlorn. Elephanta, the immediate goal of the chance visitor to Bombay, scarcely exists for those who live here. The great rough-hewn statues still gaze out, but it is over an alien world. East and West have met on these islands, and the former is being driven reluctantly away to the mainland, of which, however, nothing will dispossess her. So reluctantly, indeed, that even now the two great hemispheres live side by side, and the East, at any rate, hardly sees the inconsistency. Do you want a proof? The great modern reservoirs of Malabar Hill are netted over lest gruesome morsels drop from the claws of the heavy-flying vultures of the Towers of Silence. Nor is this all. Beside the pepals and palmettos of the curving shore the dull, heavy smell of burnt wood—and of some other burning thing as well—

foists raw India upon the civilised senses of half-Europeanised Bombay, and the frock-coated native with a heavily-tinselled cap of velvet, who, with a kick, has just helped his dead father's soul to escape from the charred prison of the skull, climbs into a first-class carriage at Marine Lines Station, just across the way from the burning-ghat, unconscious of any inconsistency. Nothing, indeed, is inconsistent in Bombay, except Elephanta, and she perhaps does not count. She has seen too much of too many peoples.

Bombay lives fiercely from day to day, accepting all as grist that comes to her ever-turning temse. Her very architecture is restless and feverish. Who but those who live hectically in a kind of Asian Vanity Fair would have reared the strange piles of the Victoria Terminus and the Taj-Mahal Hotel? These are the true emblems of Bombay. Despite her magnificence she is but a caravanserai and a starting-place, and you scarcely need to move off the white and blue floors of the gigantic rest-house on the Apollo Basin—shades of Arjumand, they are composed of mud and crockery chips!—to know all that it imports to know of this roaring metropolis and clearing-house of the commerce of five continents. Hither comes as much of the bazaar

A Bhairagi.

[Facing page 8.

as you may believe is characteristic of Bombay. Here for a night or two all Anglo-India stays, drives out under the "Queen's Necklace," round the bay, eats its last of French cookery. Generals and subalterns, collectors, commissioners, Americans and clerks, globe-trotters, parsons, planters, men who remember, as of yesterday, the Ripon riots in Calcutta in 1883, men who, as young men, lined the road along which dead Mayo passed in state in 1873—all come in their turn. But no one stays. The incoming and the outgoing tides surge and jostle in the cabined confines of the gate, and all alike are strangers in a strange city.

Last year the Prince of Wales invested her with a transient importance, and with a population which taxed even her wide spaces to accommodate, but when the splendid week had passed Bombay heard again as the dominant note of her existence only the thrumming mills and hoarse cries of the exchange and of the market, which had never ceased within her all the while. She is inscrutable. In some ways—and those not the best, perhaps—she needs insistent care and attention. Her boasted title of the First of Indian Cities rings through the Indian Ocean, but here Death is always a near acquaintance, and plague and famine close companions. Here, too, the up-washed vagrancy of the Arabian Sea is thrown ashore to mingle with the unballasted human trash of all races, with all the flotsam and jetsam that silts downwards to a congenial Smyrna in a farther Levant. If you seek for romance in Bombay you must seek it among those who cannot get away from her; you must demand it of the Thagi and Dacoity department or of the slum missionary.

You may find someone to tell you that strange tale of how, not many years ago, an earnest young police official caused to be arrested an aged mendicant, whose bodily marks corresponded with those of one who had been "wanted" by Government for forty years. He wired to Simla. Wise, entirely wise, the Viceroy "cleared the line" and made the telegraph wires hot in the urgency of his counter-order, "Release at once." Now the man—so he said, and so the police believed—was no other than Nana Sahib himself. True or false, it is not uncharacteristic of the place that that dark and restless soul, hounded from place to place, seeking friends, adherents, believers, and finding none from Tibet to Satara, should at last be drawn inevitably into the tortuous currents of Bombay, where, as in London, a man may hide himself beyond all search, and it was akin to Bombay that here of all places in the East the last transitory glimpse may have been caught, as a diseased and beggared outcast, of the infamous figure of the last century. Herein alone is Bombay's romantic side. Of history and pageant she has little, and to-day she is as free from sentiment as the notices in the halls of her hotels. She has her own business to do, and she has no time to waste. She builds hugely, because it is convenient to transact business in ample offices. But she waters the streets and plants trees with coloured leaves for the same reason as that for which she accumulates meaningless finials, unnecessary balustrades, silly rosettes, and gratuitous cusps on the outside of her buildings, and paints their insides with fearsome pre-Victorian patterns and glazes their windows with large lozenges of green and yellow and red glass. Some-one has told her it is right to do these things, and she has done them, only too glad to shift to others the responsibility. But after her own interests she looks well enough, and there is not a port in the East, perhaps not a port in the West either, whose prosperity is founded on such stable foundations as those which the scanty subsoil of this overcrowded island-spit supplies.

An Indian Railway Journey.

One goes so slowly on an Indian line and, on the whole, so easily, that one can watch the passing landscape as comfortably as from a stage-coach. And there is always something to see. Early in the first cool dawn you may raise yourself on one elbow to look out across the purple earth to where the first dull crimson and gold is gathering in the East, but even then you will never be early enough to have anticipated the day's labour. The European conception of the Oriental as an easy-going and indolent man, content to get his work done with the least possible exertion to himself, is only a half truth. It is founded on the fact that the Englishman in India, to a great extent, still keeps to his home hours of work and rest, and, therefore, is busiest and most abroad when the Asiatic rests, and is asleep or indoors during the long cool dark hours, when Indian work in field and city alike is being done. The work in the fields may not be hard, but it is day-long and year-long; even the children do their little share from morning to night. Here, in a little plot of millet, bald of even a stalk in places, and stunted from end to end, is a crazy machan or bird-scarer's perch, like a stork's nest on four bamboo supports, whereon crouches a seven-year-old boy beneath the scanty shade of a ragged piece of soiled cloth. He has no rattle, but he cries out shrilly as a flight of felon birds swoops down with the orderly flight of telegraph wires on his charge. A small store of stones he employs shrewdly, and to his youthful mind the goose and the peacock have no sacrosanctity above an inquisitive pair of mynas or a flight of hungry linnets. The train itself helps him not at all. In a surprisingly short time the birds and beasts of India have come to accept the train as a noisy but good-natured kind of elephant, that never looks either to his right or to his left or leaves the beaten track. Even the palpitating lizards do but flick themselves a yard or two from the thundering flanges.

Between the railway line itself and the wire fencing there generally is a no-man's land of grey, unfertile soil, a gritty slope on which the ak plant flourishes. This is your veritable emblem of India. With its thick glaucous leaves, its stalk-clinging white and purple blossoms, it grows as luxuriantly at Landi Kotal as at Palk Straits. No desert soil is too dry, no rock cleft too poor, to nourish this curious shrub; there is not a poorly-developed specimen, not even a dried or browned leaf of the ak from one end of India to the other. Go up to a plant in the most torrid stretch of waterless stone and sand in the peninsula, in such a place that nothing else—not even the white-flowered "gos," its nearest rival—can survive, and snap a stem between your fingers. Instantly there is an outrush of white viscous fluid; the very leaves are milky reservoirs as well. You had better not rub your eyes with your fingers afterwards. It is one of the inexplicable freaks of Nature, and were it less common, would be cultivated under a Latin name in hothouses at home. For it is a handsome plant, though, unhonoured and unsung, it remains the pariah flower of India. Rubber can be made of this ak juice. But a commercial expert once gravely explained to me that the reason why there were not likely to be great results from its employment for this purpose, was that the resultant rubber was totally inelastic.

Hard by, if the ground be poor enough, will

be the handsome datura, with its large white trumpets amid the strongly-cut deep green foliage. It is a fine weed, and, like the yellow turwar yonder, prefers ruins and dead soils to thrive among. But an ineradicable habit of the Indian peasantry renders it unpopular. They cunningly extract from it a simple and efficacious poison, and any Assistant-Commissioner will confess that the "snake-bite" returns of his district are often swollen out of recognition by the victims of the datura. Beyond this little strip of desert the interest of the land begins.

While still near Bombay, travel in India will seem cast in pleasant and fertile spots. Beneath Salsette and by Kalyan the deep-fringed bananas and feathering cocoanuts rise from such ponds as are illustrated in the geography books of the nursery, and the rich avenues of shisham that shade the village streets sweep past with a dignity that is almost English. The crops of maize are six feet high, and the whole face of the country seems sopping with excess of rain. But the reversing stations near Igatpuri will put a sudden end to the rich promise of the western slopes of the Ghauts. East of these historic mountains the drought of last year is apparent. One cannot wonder that a dry season means death for thousands here. Out to the very horizon the dry, wasted plains of India, seamed with arid water-courses, stretch; to the visitor the lack of fertility will seem to change but little from end to end of the sub-continent, except in those districts which are fed by the gigantic water distributions of man's making. A wheeling vision of dust and drought is in most years the prevailing sight.

The scene from an Indian railway carriage window may include almost everything that is most characteristic in the Empire, the tortured waste of waterless nullahs by the Chambal—the fleeting vision of the pearl-like Taj across the river, with which the East Indian Railway closes its long mileage into Agra—the "karroo" of Bikanir—the green tropical vegetation of the Darjiling Railway, crowned by the Himalayan snows—the lush, rank jungle of Madras—the iron thunderings across the sand-bordered trickles that at this season represent the five rivers of the north-west—the waterfalls and ferns of the Khandala gradients—the grinding curves and everlasting smoke-bound tunnels of the Simla Railway, and a hundred other scenes, all true and transient pictures of different sides of Indian life, are there for him to see; but the vision that he and most

THE ELEPHANTS' BATHING POOL

Indian travellers will remember best is none of these. It is such a scene as one has seen ten hundred times, the dusty road crossing the track beneath the dusty bebel tree on the one side, and the dusty "padwan" on the other. A single iron rail across it checks a little party. who stare as the train goes by—a woman drawing her sari's edge across her lips, while she holds in upon her hips her naked child astraddle; perhaps an older child running up and waving a welcome to the carriages, and a man attending to one of the two bullocks lest it swerve. Perhaps a pad-footed camel, heavily laden on either side with packs of coarse sacking; perhaps a ruth or zenana bullock-cart, closely veiled against both curiosity and the sun. On the dipping telegraph-wires a green parakeet and a flash of white feathers, as two mynas tumble upon the dusty ground with a spread of wings—the eternal whine of a Persian water-wheel, that can hardly be seen under the shade of a dusty banyan across an allotment of dry plough-marks. The sun beats down fiercely upon the scene, and the bullocks blink their fly-ringed eyes in the glare, and the drifting red dust floats from under our wheels upon them all as we watch and go by. A cactus hedge, like a line of escaped sea monsters, holds up its green claws and bat-like hands, all unnaturally blossomed at the edge with yellow flowers, and the raw smell of acacia wood comes from a little fire beside the stone posts of the railway fencing. The man who is cooking there does not deign even to turn his head over his shoulder to see us pass. The picture is gone as soon as it has come, and the dull succession of dry red fields, surface-scratched and bare, succeeds again, broken only by a rare village, or the muddy stagnant pool in which a water buffalo wallows, his nostrils alone standing out above the scum of the water. And then every two or three hours the crowded and confused panorama of a great railway station, the huddled multitudes lying like dim sheep at night, and pressing and shouting like another Babel all the day ; the long-drawn cries of "Pan bhéree-e-e" from the platform hucksters hurrying up and down, the strange meetings over a hasty meal at wayside stations of men from Seistan or Mogok, the curious knowledge of obscure junction villages, where half a day has to be wasted before a train comes in. Well do I remember one such occasion.

Between Raichur and Adoni the combings of the rake of Allah have been swept together into heaps and ranges of bare rock and sun-baked hills of blackened lumber. It is a bare country. Aloe hedges shut in both sides of the line, their tall flowers seeming by their very shape to mock the telegraph poles beside them. Yellow mimosas, or bebel thorns, flourish in the dry soil, and where there is a patch of moisture spiky palmettos and cocoanuts spring; maize grows poorly in such places, too, and you will sometimes see a string of child-herded buffaloes slowly passing along for their evening mud-bath outside the village. That is all, and of all the dreary stations in this land Wadi is the dreariest. It is in Hyderabad and a junction with the line owned by the Nizam. It also has a refreshment room, wherein one dines on the way between Madras and Bombay. But conceive it! There is a blistering length of platform set between the glittering silver of the railway lines—(nothing ever rusts here). The station consists of the few necessary official rooms, and, if I remember, there is a corrugated iron roof, and there is a big water-tank, upborne by iron pillars, for the use of the engines. There is a triple dripping water-carrier for the use of the natives, and a bougainvillea blazes insolently with its crude hot magenta against the wide desert sky All round the wilderness lies hot and empty. To the west there are half a dozen ramshackle houses of mud in which the railway workmen have to live.

Some years ago I spent a day there. Coming up from Hampi, I had to join the train that ran through Wadi somewhere about midnight. I shall never forget that day. One hour seemed like six. There was absolutely no single thing to do from one minute to the next. I had no book. There was nothing to shoot, there was nothing to sketch. The heat sweltered along the empty station, and every now and again great "boofs" of searingly hot air stirred the leaf-flowers of the bougainvillea. The shadow of the overhead roof made the heat just tolerable. One could not put one's hand upon anything an inch beyond its sharply-cut purple shadow. The sixth telegraph pole north and south crawled with the mirage. I went to see the station-master. "Do they keep you long here?" I asked.

"Not very. I am asking for an exchange at once, though."

"You surprise me," I said grimly.

"I want it," he said, "for two reasons. One," he went on, "you can imagine for yourself," and he shrugged his arms out while a hotter blast than usual stirred along the platform. "The other," said he, crossing his legs, "is different. Things got so monotonous here that a little time ago I thought I'd have a joke. So I wrote an account of a cricket match played here between the Wadi Junction eleven and a visiting team from Adoni."

I looked at him. Cricket teams at Wadi. Mark Tapley could scarcely have done better.

"Yes," he went on ruminatively, "I did the whole thing well. I was modest about myself too, and I sent it to the newspapers, and they all printed it. Well, after that, I had these cricket matches once a week, and after a bit I gave the averages of the team. But I did not reckon upon one thing. Thanks. The sporting editor of some Bombay paper began talking of the 'hitherto untapped resources of this well-known sporting centre,' and he suggested that the gentleman at the head of the bowling averages should be given a chance for—what do you suppose?—the presidency match. It is forty miles to their boundary. Well," he said, "what was I to do? A letter came in asking whether it were possible for this bowler to get away for a day or two for some trial match. That I stopped all right," he continued. "I wrote officially as myself to say that he could not be spared, but it left me in a hole. I could not very well stop sending the reports in, so I determined to reduce his form. That is not so easy, you know, with a bowler."

"But it was no use. The thing had spread," he went on, "and I got other letters, challenges, special terms offered for cricketing outfits, and, worst of all, a man has just written to me, and says that he has started on a round of cricketing visits during his holiday, and asks if I can put him up at the club here. Club!" repeated the station-master, with a withering accent of sarcasm. "And he would like a day or two's play with our well-known local team. He is due here in about ten days. Of course it is not so much that he will expose my little fun, but the poor devil has probably arranged his tour, and will have lost two or three days somewhere else. That," concluded the station-master, "is why I want to go away."

I had no solution to suggest.

"A curious thing," went on the station-master—"how easily you can take in people who flatter themselves they know India. Why, every soul in the offices of the *West Coast Clarion* must pass through this blighted hole half a dozen times a year, yet they swallowed my cricket stories without turning a hair. Gad!" he added, "I'd like to have 'em down here for a week. Club, indeed!"

We looked out over the empty bald bare grit of the South Indian desert plateau. Forty miles away there was a blue line of hills. Between them and us there was absolutely no single thing to break the quivering horizon line. If we had looked on the other side of the station we should have seen the same thing. Conversation flagged. Even the refreshment room was shut up between train times, probably to save from inebriety the prisoner-passengers of Wadi. Merely to break the monotony I walked out along the line in the sun. A few lizards flicked anxiously into crannies in the baked earth. That was all the movement in the landscape, except the effervescence of the mirage. There was the peace of Hades over everything. I went back to the deserted patch of purple shadow under the iron roof, and immediately the least expected thing in the world happened.

The station-master, watching a far distant-crawling speck, said, "That's a special." And some time after up to the station there came a train, carrying a travelling circus and menagerie. Nine-feet elephants looked plaintively over the tops of the trucks. Panthers and ounces growled behind bars. Horses, pie-bald and skew-bald, whinnied in their boxes, and a flight of graceful white-and-tan collies were loosed from a truck on to the platform. It was the quaintest sight you might imagine, and after the nice beasts there descended upon the platform the European men and women of the show. The men were in shirt-sleeves, dirty—oh, very dirty!—collars, slippers, and a two-day growth of beard. They had perhaps not washed for more than two days. Their language was unpleasant, their habits were similar. The ladies of the troupe—but no! They all made at once for the refreshment room. It was a relief to go back to the beasts, and I ask you whether there ever was such a contrast as that between the aching, empty levels of the deserted Wadi desert and these specimens of Western civilisation. There was a great bronzed Sikh on the platform, when, after disputing the bill with such expletive energy that the Babu in charge of the refreshment room gave up the struggle, these representatives of the Sahib-log came out again on to the plaftorm, and one by one challenged comparison with the clean-cut, aristocratic features of this "nigger"—as they called him. I felt inclined to go up and apologise to the Sikh. But I forbore. I remembered another occasion, many hundred miles away, when the last touch was put to an incident, which reflected little credit upon a few Englishmen, by the respectful sympathy which an austere, hook-nosed Pathan rissaldar expressed with the humiliation which his own clean-cut, resourceful white officer must then be feeling. In a few minutes the train re-started, and the travelling company rumbled off across the waste. I wish they had left one of the collies behind them. In ten minutes the desert had resumed its barren solemnity, and the station-master said, "Talking about that cricket team——"

Udaipur.

ELSEWHERE in Indian India there is magnificence enough of human construction. Vast fortresses there are, and jewelled suites of women's apartments, the pomp of isolated tower or crowded audience chamber, the ostentatious piety of marble mosque and gilt-roofed temple, or the homes of that grim and austere faith which was content to burrow out dark Cyclopean halls in the living rock, and worship three hundred feet below the grasses wilting in the sunshine on the mountain side. But alone at Udaipur is there in its perfection the fairy palace of one's childhood, just such a long cataract of marble terraces and halls falling into the waters of a mountain-encircled lake, as the illustrator of an Andrew Lang fairy book delights to draw.

It is an old story that Viceroy after Viceroy has come to Udaipur revolving in his mind schemes for bringing this lonely capital to date, and devising methods for the utilisation of Udaipur's natural

Chitor.

[*Facing page* 26.

advantages of wood and water. Viceroy after Viceroy from Simla or Calcutta had expressed a hope that those modern improvements which have been adopted to their vast material benefit by other States might find a home here also. But Viceroy after Viceroy has gone back from Udaipur well content to leave her as she is, unspoiled and unimproved, recognising that dynamo and driving band are poor substitutes for the splendid pattern of old-world chivalry and courteous tradition which this lovely lake-side palace sets, not to Mewar and Rajputana only, of which the Maharana is the undisputed overlord, but to all India alike. The lord of all these white marbles, blue waters, and attendant hills has no equal in our empire. It is true that the State of Mewar, over which he rules, is neither the largest nor the richest even among his kith and kin of Rajputana: strategically Udaipur is a backwater; moreover, it contains no such holy spots as half a dozen other principalities may claim; it is only within the last ten years that a railway has enabled a traveller to visit it in comparative comfort; the Government of India has never been caused a pang of anxiety by anything that has ever taken place within the borders of the State. Yet Udaipur stands alone and unrivalled in India by virtue of India's most characteristic and iron-bound law. Were free election to be made to-morrow among the native competitors for the kingship of India, no one would dare to stand against the Maharana of Udaipur. Islam might gnash its teeth, but the odds are great, and the Pathans are but an unstable foundation for an empire. For Udaipur is the two hundred-and-fortieth descendant in right line from the Sun, and primate and pontifex secular among all who hold the Hindu faith. From a hundred walls looks down the Rana's emblem —gules, the Sun in his splendour, or. Timidly do even the haughtiest claim kinship with him. Once upon a time the great Jang Bahadur sent down twenty-seven thousand maunds of grain to the relief of his famine-stricken "cousins" in Rajputana. The word "cousin" is vague enough in Hindostan, and the gift was accepted. Had the Maharana known that Nepal was on the strength of this kinship daring to use his celestial insignia, the tribute would have been rejected as an insult, for even the difference between the sun and the moon is not as great as that between "suraj" and "chandar" in this genealogy.

But Udaipur would remain princess among the cities of India were it but a bania or a sweeper

From the Palace : Udaipur.

[*Facing page* 28.

caste which reigned beside the Pichola lake. Walls, indeed, and a grim bastioned gateway or two, a vast and blood-stained record of gallantry, and a warlike tradition—that still finds its echo in the tulwar which every man carries in his hand to this day, even though he doubles it up with an umbrella —all these are here, and at Chitor, yet Udaipur remains dainty and feminine, as no other city is in hither or farther India. She is approached wearily. Even now the train from Chitorgarh labours along the bare, rising plains of Rajputana, with a heat and a dust and a tardiness which are no unfit substitutes for those brambles and spines which of old have always beset the palace of a sleeping princess. Few turn aside from the beaten track of India's indicated sights to visit remote Udaipur—yet Udaipur is worth many another tourist resort. She lies remote and unhackneyed, hedged about with plains above plains, in which the only colour is that of a jay's wing or of a blue convolvulus draping a dead thorn bush; all else is grey, dun, rusty, and clogged, save the cactus hedges that stand up between plot and plot too straight and smooth to catch the trailing dust as deeply as the other vegetation. But at last the railway station, respectfully distant from the city walls, is reached, and, after a couple of miles along the road, the dak bungalow beside the walls also.

There are many things that are worth a visit in Udaipur, but the lake is the first and final attraction. It is almost a pity to go over the palace. Nothing could ever come up to the exquisite suggestion of its outside, and that, because its landward side is choked with mean houses, is only to be well seen from the island-dotted waters of Pichola. Of these islands Jag Mandar and Jag Newas are the most important. Both are almost entirely covered with white marble summer palaces, over which a few tall palms and vivid bananas lift themselves from the cloistered gardens inside. From either there is to be had a view of the Sun-child's palace which explains the attention and lavish expense which they have enjoyed at the hands of the children of Mewar. There is a terrace on Jag Mandar—just above the steps upon which the clear water dances transparently and the alligators sometimes come—from which the huge building is seen at its best. Tier above tier the snowy walls and terraces rise from the very ripples of the lake, where under the kiss of the wind their reflection makes a matted tangle of white. Here and there the whiteness of the half-translucent architecture is relieved by a touch of

Jag Mandar.

[*Facing page 30.*

green where a banyan or a group of acacias rises from a walled-in garden-plot, but the same quick white, of half a hundred shades and values, argent in the sun and veiled-blue in the shadows, spreads along the palace wall or points itself into the dome and pinnacle of the roof, till the upper line cuts the blue of the air, white from end to end of the thousand feet of the palace sky-line, save and except just where, at one end, an audacious and flaring bougainvillea leans in lambent magenta and dark olive-green over the topmost and most secluded court of all—white, white, and, from end to end, white.

You will be rowed along the river frontage, and your cicerone—whom you must have with you, as the privilege of roving about on Pichola is subject to a special permit and to this disability—will try and make you land at Jag Newas, the second of these islet palaces. But you will be wise to refuse. Let your boatmen rather row you past Nao and Lal ghats, bathing steps that lie northward to the dam. Here, in irregular echelons—broken by gravelled slopes, like Arjankura, down which the patient oxen come all day with the bhisties to have their leather water-skins filled; by the uncompromising square pipal-overhung terrace of a temple, from which an everlasting drum bangs, and the threshold is spotted with orange marigolds; by the blank wall of some Royal prince's residence—the marble steps which the bathers and the washers use, stretch out and stretch on for half a mile. Close under the King's Palace is the first of them, Pipli, hard by the moorings of the triple-storeyed State barges. The men bathe stolidly and alone, each one absorbed in attention to ritual. It is a religious duty with them, a matter to be carried out with exactitude and scruple, and a man will not notice you as you come near upon the water. The women chatter much in groups and wash clothes betimes; what with the clothes they have cast off and those that lie a-drying on the upper steps, they make up a rich picture in the morning shade beneath the temple walls. The children enjoy themselves alone and spatter and squeal and choke in the shallows. Across the way, by Hanuman's ghat, a cormorant sits expectant on a half-submerged post, and at its feet a heavy tortoise of a hundred and fifty pounds slowly turns over at water-level.

I remember a time when the Pichola Lake presented a different sight indeed. Beautiful as Udaipur is at any hour, and in any season, there is a well-remembered tradition, that when a Viceroy

UDAIPUR.

or member of the Imperial house visits her, the town and lake-front, forts, bridges, ghats, islands, and terraces shall all, that night, be outlined with fire.

It is easy to waste adjectives on such a sight, but, in sober truth, there cannot be, there can never have been elsewhere in the world, such a spectacle as the Pichola Lake presents when its quick surface reflects the quiet lights which trace in points of fire, the steps and string courses, lintels, jambs, roofs, domes, cupolas, and arched cloisters of four miles of architecture. There is much, perhaps, to be said against the custom. Next morning, remember, Udaipur lies out bedraggled and soiled with a million smoky patches on her snow-white walls, the waters of the lake are grey with soot and iridescent with spilled oil, and the lovely island palaces are defiled with smoked patches along every sill and string-course. Still, there must have been an ugly aftermath even in the most splendid days of Florentine or Roman festivals, and at the time the beauty of these persistent lines of light, daintily ruffled by the quiet night airs, is beyond words. Later on, in the evening after the Maharana's state dinner is over, when above the dots of fire the shearing rockets curve and bear coloured fruits in mid-heaven, and huge set-pieces, half-smothered and wholly improved by bulging volumes of amber smoke, crackle out in indistinguishable figures and lay coloured pathways over the rippling waters, the brilliancy and barbarism of the gorgeous sight seems the one finale needed to round off the faery perfection of Udaipur.

But on such a night, though beyond question barbaric in Oriental splendour, one touch of genius, sheer genius, saves the whole glittering scene from that colour of ostentation that might have been feared. There, where the mighty mass of the Maharana's palace rises sheer above the lake, there where most display would be expected, not a spark glitters except a single row of lights, marking the parapet line of the central block, rising square two hundred and fifty feet out of the water. All else is dark, and one rather feels the great palace to be there than knows it, though at its foot low festoons of lamps light red-carpeted stairs down to the water, which all day have been a solitary splash of crimson on the vast white building.

But on other days of sunshine take a word of advice. Life is good enough on the water. Nothing on the land is quite worth the trouble of going to see, not even the famous pig-feeding at the end of

The Royal Palace, Udaipur.

[*Facing page* 34.

the lake. Not a room in the main Palace or in the water pavilions in the lake is worth it. Within this exquisite dream of fresh white marble are rooms that must be seen to be believed. I have no hesitation in saying that one room is without rival on earth for the eye-searing taste displayed in it. It is about forty feet by twenty, and from the walls project low pillars and rough-edged plaster arches. The whole of the walls and arches is mustard yellow distemper. There is a deep frieze of atrocious German "della Robbia" plaques. The pillars are of the same material, each one a tub-like achievement of the Fatherland. From the centre of the ceiling, over a round table draped with chenille, descends a chandelier of strange form, vast and clumsy. All the glass thereon is petunia-coloured and engraved with "scenes." The furniture, of a pre-Victorian gilt description, is upholstered in frayed magenta silk brocade. But the springs are coming through, and it will be necessary to re-cover at least the settee soon—one wonders what colour will be selected. It is a good rule never to visit the modernised rooms of an Oriental palace, but Udaipur—Udaipur, "last, loneliest, loveliest, exquisite, apart"—is perhaps, in this respect, the very worst example that can be found.

One turns in towards the Pipli Ghat again, and as one passes idly beneath the pipal that overhangs the bank, a flight of seven pigeons dashes out across the surface of the water to the sunset, piercing the thick leaves like a salvo of round shot, and my lord the elephant, under his crazy thatch of long grasses, takes off and eats the turban of matted fodder that has served him all day as a sun-bonnet. The walls of the palace change colour from lemon-yellow through orange to a faint rose, and thence through amethyst to a dull dead-leaden white, as the last hues die out of the sky. One has to find one's way home through the royally luxurious Durbar gardens, past the open-air wheelwright's establishment, past the tortuous and crowded lanes of gallantly-painted houses and crazy shops, till we make the great gateway, and emerge into the cold, clear evening air, and see the massive bastions and battlements of Sasnisargarh beyond the scanty lights of the dak bungalow.

On the Lake: Udaipur.

[*Facing page* 36.

Jaipur.

You cannot imagine for yourselves the capital of Rajputana unless you bring visibly before the eye of the mind that city which, by order of Suleiman-ben-Daoud, was carried bodily away by Jinns, and planted as it stood in the midst of the desert. North, south, and east, the high scarps of the protecting mountain ranges rise fair and steep, fortified with creeping lines of masonry; but the wide waste of sand which stretches out westward lies hidden behind them also—merciless, unsympathising, encroaching. The City of Victory offers a vain and doomed resistance. Five miles away, among the mountains to the north, Amber, the old city, waits, patient and ruined, for the day to come when the long-delayed tide of desert sand shall sweep round into the recess where Jaipur hides, and the dainty gardens and wide pink-washed streets of balconied and latticed houses shall at last become part and parcel of the great Indian desert. Even now the long levels stretch interminably, dry and arid, choked with drifted heaps of grit where a fold in the ground or a scorched boulder has arrested the ever-running skein of wind-blown sand, and seamed with the thirsty nullahs where no plant blows. Only a few bebel thorns find beside the track a scanty catchment of water in the hollows dug out to provide embankment for the fiery rails, and low clouds of the loose-petalled wild cassia alternates a pungent yellow with the faint lilac and grey-green of the inevitable ak plant.

Inside a sheltered nook in the mountains of Rajputana, where the bare spurs of the Amber ridge thrust out huge sand groynes into the wilderness, Jai Singh built him his new home and set it about with wide and metalled roads and orderly squares, and all the green comfort of a garden town. From a distance Jaipur lies hidden amid its own foliage. Only here and there the high bastions of the city gates, the dainty finials and cupolas of the palace or of Jacob's Museum, or the curving edges of a flame-like temple tower, rise high over the sea of banyan and neem and straggling acacia. But year by year the vanguard of the desert creeps up from the south-west nearer and nearer into the very mouth of this haven of refuge. For Jaipur lies unprotected and assailable from just that one quarter from which the danger comes. Her green-robed squares and avenues, the compounds which surround her houses, her gardens and her gallant walks, spotting and slashing the sea of stone and tile and mortar, are only a real mirage. The Maharaja is but playing the game that Mrs. Partington once played, and the ocean of the desert will some day win to the foot of the hills, and the broad town of green and ochre and pink will be as Tadmor. Even now the first ripples of that tide are seen in the twelve-foot bridle-track of four-inch dust with which the roads are fringed upon the right hand and upon the left; already the very palace courts are scenes of miniature cyclones, and the sills of the wayside temple gates are banked up flush with a ramp of white dust. The very trees that look so well from the heights above, drive their hard-pressed roots through dust only to deeper dust, and so, perhaps, to some low stratum where they may suck some scanty moisture still left from last season's rains. In the public gardens, the flowers rise from thick layers and blankets of the soft and silky powdering, and there is not a leaf or a blade of grass from end to end of the city which is not permanently fringed and coated with the white threat of the oncoming wilderness without. Always the veil, thinner now and then again thicker, hangs in the air twelve feet high; once or twice a day a dust-storm drives a stinging haze of particles which penetrate like a smell through the very walls and windows of the house.

Up on the deserted hills, Amber still resists the subtle teeth of age and neglect. Indeed, were a palace all that is needed, the Maharaja of Jaipur might transfer himself to his old capital with as little delay as attends the flitting of the Viceroy from Calcutta to Simla year by year. All is here still—the courts of audience and the gardens of repose, the women's apartments and the long galleries for the men and beasts. Even to this day the temple is served as diligently as ever, and the early visitor to Amber may still see the morning sacrifice to Kali hustled into the sacred domain—a goat, dyed blue upon its head and neck, and vaguely resisting the efforts of the priest's acolytes to shepherd him in these unwonted paths. Excepting always the Imperial palaces of India, there is not in the peninsula a more exquisite structure of marble inlaid with precious and semi-precious stones, of sandal-wood inlaid with ebony and ivory, than this deserted

Amber Palace.

[*Facing page* 40.

home of long dead and forgotten chieftains. Indeed, the story goes that Jehangir himself, the pettiest of soul of all the Mogul Emperors, sent peremptory orders that his vassal's beautiful home should be pulled down, as being more beautiful than his own. But his emissary arrived at Amber only to find the exquisite carvings of pillar and corbel and bracket plastered and overlaid with an inch-thick coat of rough cement and whitewash, and he could only return and report with amazement to his Imperial master that rumour had strangely exaggerated the beauties of Mirza Raja's new palace. Amber city needs far more concern. At a distance its streets and walls seem fairly stout though roofless, but a hundred and eighty years of neglect have worked far more havoc in poorer homes of sun-dried brick and loose stone than in the marble and sandstone palace. Everywhere the indefatigable acacia has rooted itself, and the long, lithe trails of convolvulus and karela help, in their lesser way, the work of disintegration.

In Jaipur itself, where East jostles West, at times you may still see the last remnants of the old Indian sports, unchanged since days long before those of the Mohammedan emperors. Now and again, in the noonday heat, you may have seen a leopard crouching along beside its master—querulous, uncertain, half-timid, heavily hooded with blue silk, and finding the trimmed stone of the pavement maddeningly hot beneath its silent pads. But it is a different animal when at last after a tedious stalk of a herd of black buck, the leopard is unhooded from the whining bullock-cart and left to his own work. In all the world there is little left so savage and so beautiful as this steel-springed cat when he scents his quarry. In a flash he has dropped to the plain, belly-flat upon the hot stones, while he works his way to a ten-inch patch of a sage brush, all elbows, and seemingly but four inches above the ground. You may see the trail of him as he goes. From one bush he makes for another or a fold of ground. One watches him with a touch of his own silence, though the little caravan of bullock carts must still be kept moving lest their stopping should alarm the buck. So it goes on, this yellow devil edging himself nearer and nearer to his chosen prey, till while yet fifty yards away the buck raises his head. Whether he localises his danger at once or not, there is no chance of stalking him a yard further, and the cheetah makes his dash. The buck is gone like a flash of lightning. There is not a sound on either side. Two of the fastest animals on earth—the cheetah is beyond all question the swiftest—engage in a life-and-death race. It is soon over, for if the cheetah does not bring his prey down in two hundred yards he throws up the chase and returns ignominiously to his master. If he catches the buck there is an ugly finale of jetting life-blood and convulsed limbs and glazing eyes, interfered with by the cheetah's master, who brings a huge wooden spoon filled with blood and entrails, which he forcibly substitutes for the buck itself under the still sucking muzzle of the unsated leopard. But whether he catch his prey or not, the cheetah's flight over the ground for two hundred yards is a thing for which alone it is almost worth while to go to Jaipur.

Other barbaric sports still hold their own here. All one afternoon there be animal-fighting in the Maharaja's arena. Every male beast, and not a few birds also, is here pitted against his own kind; stags, goats, buffaloes, rams, boars—everything that has the power to fight is here brought into the lists, and anyone who has once heard the sound of the meeting of two fresh and keen rams will remember it, with a headache, to this day. Little harm is actually done; most of these duels terminate by the exhaustion of both sides, while the quails, cocks, and partridges seem positively to enjoy an occasional set-to in public. Nearer home still, the alligators may be fed with lumps of raw meat in the huge rectangular tank. At first you will hardly believe that there are any of the brutes there at all, but the high call of their keeper at a little ghat on one side of the reservoir will, after a time, cause little whirlpools on the surface of the water, and a horny head will rise for a moment, sink, and reappear a few yards nearer. When once they have been collected and lie at the water's edge, the food is thrown, and half-a-dozen "muggers" snap at the gory morsels. You might think that an alligator was an unhefty brute until one of them rushes the ramp of the ghat for a good twelve feet and snaps its jaws together, a yard away from your trouser ends, upon some carelessly dropped lump of stringy meat. After all, it is but a poor substitute for an erring wife: the stomachs of the older brutes are full of glass bangles.

Yes, one has only to scratch Jaipur to realise that the modern commercialism and dull municipal excellence of the city is hardly more than a veneer, like the dust which lies so heavily.

There is a strange charm which comes out at sunset by reason of this very mantle of drought made visible. An hour before the evening falls, one wanders through wide streets that become multitudinous as one looks, and bright with colours that only Mandalay of all places in the world can hope to rival. Scarlet and orange and pink, white, yellow and ochre, greens of strange virulence, and greens of sad restraint, copper and flame colour and orpiment, all blend themselves unerringly in the tangled skeins of colour like beds of salpiglossis in an English garden. Roadway and wide pavement—a rare thing in the East—are filled with the jostling throng through which one amazing man in a single robe of almost phosphorescent chartreuse—yellow and green mixed—makes his way, changing the colour values as he goes from group to group. Before him and his lambent aureoline-green, magenta becomes mauve and sap-green sage, and he leaves behind him a wake of mourning hues.

Here comes an elephant, going delicately in fear of his own bulk, gently scattering and sweeping humanity aside; there, a supercilious and shamble-quartered camel; bullocks grey, dun, and white, with horns of vermilion or myrtle green; a blue-hooded cheetah, padding nervously along beside his master, and always the jolting revolutions of ox-cart-wheels, innocent of tyre or axle-grease, and patched like a child's box of bricks.

The raw metal jangle of the temple bells sounds from behind the rose-red walls of lattice, pillar, arch and balcony, and from behind the ochreous plaster curtains of different planes, machicolated, crenellated, bracketed, over which hangs the acacia which finds its own way wherever man plants an Eastern plot of garden soil.

Here and there a circle gathers round a charmer or a story-teller, but the city's population mostly move quietly forward in hooded thousands, as orderly and as aimless as ever was a church parade in the Park, a kaleidoscope of moving and intertwining colour. Uncouth feudal retainers of the Maharaja, as strange to the city as oneself, blinkingly pick their way along the streets, dressed in tarnished chain-armour or quilted suits of rusty crimson. Nagas, also collected here on performance of grand serjeanty, creep in twos and threes along the by-ways, their plumed caps and two-handed swords, scabbardless and quivering like a flame, stared at by country cousins as oddly habited as themselves. Agate and apricot, geranium and garnet, all hues of red float past. More magnificent than all, there comes an elephant fresh painted for to-morrow's state, in geometrical patterns of magenta green and yellow, and over all of his bulk, a huge wrap of half-inch cloth of gold falls like a carpet from his shoulder to his feet. But he is soon lost to sight in the gathering dusk and dust, for the evening has come.

Before one knows it the nightly mystery of the Indian west has spread, and the flaming crimson curtain hangs behind a swaying veil of what no longer looks like dust, but rather a gauze through which the hardly recognisable shapes distorted in the coloured gloom move unsteadily to and fro. Mountainous bundles, stalks of millet or of maize, move forward of their own motion, betrayed only by the whining protest of the hidden wheels, obscuring, as they pass, the little fires which dot the pavements, each burning high and clear as the red daylight dies.

The colours vanish in the veil of fire-opal red that blinds and blends all edges and all hues. Only, straight above one, is the sky still blue, though there, too, the shafts of amethyst are striking home. The dinner fires gleam brightly and well against the drifting clouds of whitened and half-translucent smoke, but two shades deeper than the mist itself. The dust sways and glides in coloured lines, and the sharp aromatic smell of burning acacia mingles with the bitterness of the dust in the nostrils.

Dust, indeed, it is no longer. It is the glory of Jaipur. Not for the clearest view on earth would one exchange the panorama of misty, white, wood-fed flames beside the roads, and the hardly seen staging of Oriental lattice and verandah which now and then frames a silhouetted figure in a doorway. The suspended splendour of the sky sinks for a moment, only to rise again with that inexplicable volcanic after-glow which just now supplies the self-appointed augurs of the bazaar with material for dismal forebodings of death and pestilence and flight before the enemy—all due, needless to say, to the strange tenderness of the Englishman for the useless girl babies that come in such numbers to the struggling Rajput. "In my day——," but he is a known liar, and the story dies away on his lips. The crowd seems to sink into the ground again, and the loneliness of the road which runs out westward to the Residency is emphasised as tree after tree swings by in silence, save for its load of shrill cicadas grinding their knives in every bough, and the never ending refrain of the frogs—for all the world like the sound of a stone thrown ricocheting along thin English ice—taken up from dry pond to dry pond beside the darkening track.

Delhi.

DELHI, the mistress of every conqueror of India, Aryan or Afghan, Persian, English or Mogul, remains unconquered still. Over twenty square miles of sun-baked plain lie out the débris of her many pasts, relics of her dead and gone masters, some perfect still, some once more crumbling back into the levels of red-yellow marl that have alternately fed and housed, and fed and housed again forgotten generations of men. Yet Delhi lives. Like some huge crustacean, she has shed behind her her own outgrown habitations, as she has crawled northwards from Tughlakabad and Lalkot, through Dinpana and Ferozabad, till the long, red lizard of the Ridge barred her way, and now she suns herself, a raffle of narrow and congested byways, beneath the crimson walls of Shah Jehan's great palace-fort. But Delhi is more than her streets and temples. You may go round about her and count her towers; you may tramp from the Jumna Masjid to the Fort, from the Fort to the Pillar, from the Pillar to Humaion's Tomb and the great Minar; and when all is seen you will understand that these things do no honour to Delhi; it is Delhi that doubles their significance, and that of all that is found within her wide borders. Inscrutable and undeniable, her claim is different from that of all other towns of India, for she has no rival in greatness from the mountains to the sea, and all men know that whoso holds Delhi holds India. A wide and almost waste plain stretches along the eastern bank of a sandy expanse of river-bed. In the far distance low violet hills hem in the horizon, and almost every acre of the plain between the river and the hills bears its own monument of Delhi's bygone days. In among the tangles of thorn-bush and mimosa, where no living thing passes by save a wandering buffalo or the shadow of a kite wheeling high up in the sun, the walls and terraces of deserted temples crumble, and the white datura or the raw yellow acacia flourishes beside the altar stones. Here and there an arch springs forty feet to where a bird-borne pipal-plant slowly threatens a lingering keystone, and an azure-necked peacock scratches among the rotting stumps of last year's self-sown Indian corn.

Beyond the hard white shaded road—the only serviceable and well-kept thing in all the landscape—rises in a garden the dome of an ostentatious tomb. Some servant of an Emperor, some Emperor himself it may be, who sleeps soundly in his grave, all unconscious that the city he believed so abiding and so loyal has drifted far from him and his all-powerful dynasty, and now darkens the northward sky with the smoke of factory chimneys, and of locomotives straining across the iron-bridged Jumna. Far away to the south still stands the shaft raised by the slave-emperor from Turkestan, and underneath it the iron pillar of an earlier "conqueror of the universe" bears witness yet to its Royal maker's foolishness. Tughlakabad, hard by, is given over to the jackal and the cobra and the owl—the very bats have found in it no ceiling for their foul nestings. Lalkot lies a weed-grown fold of scattered half-hewn stone and mud; it needs an antiquarian to guess where here and there a gate may once have pierced the vaunted fortifications of old. Indraprastha is there still, but she has given up the struggle against fate, and her cornices and parapets fall unheeded across her exits and her entrances. Only the Grand Trunk Road endures between and beneath the shadows of the heavy banyans above, whose leaves are whitened daily by the dust-shuffling bullock-carts, just as when Shah Jehan's vast equipage trailed slowly in to his new capital from that old one, which had become a burden upon his heart too heavy for him to bear. A few minarets have pierced the skyline for some time, but as one follows along its clear metalled strip, Delhi itself—Delhi, that is, of to-day—rises flat and uncomely behind her long, low, fortified and battlemented walls. Outside, the glacis is clear, save for a few yellow-flowered bebels and a crumbling chaitya or two; inside there is the well-remembered jostle and stench of every native quarter of the East, and so through eight-foot thoroughfares below jutting eaves and, rarely, dirty balconies, one reaches the one great street that cleaves the town in halves, the famous Chandni Chauk.

Meagre, ramshackle houses—one-storeyed, and plastered with torn paper, their dirty blue paint smeared over decayed whitewash—lean one against the other, and expose on their vermin-haunted walls and raised floors cheap European goods or trays of fly-blown native sweets, bowls of chillies or onions, framed oleographs of gods or English princes, American nickel clocks, or scrap-iron heaps. In between them some brick and mortar missionary station puts out its nigh-hopeless appeal, or some native chemist advertises his willingness to practise indifferently the medical system of either East or West. But the real shops of the "Silver Street" are those which make little show to the public eye. You can hardly believe that those unpretentious little cabins, where the scarlet-teethed shopmen in alpaca coats smile upon you as you pass, have within call half the jewels of India. Down the middle of the Chandni Chauk runs a line of branching banyans —such as Tavernier found useful in his trade, for he says that one can judge the water of a diamond best in the dappled shade of a leafy tree—their trunks all mud below where the bhisti sprinkles, all dust above, and at the end of them, across the burnt grass of the Maidan, rise the dusty crimson walls of the fort.

There is much for a man to see in Delhi; there is even more waiting for him to understand. One might set him with muffled feet upon the gigantic courtyard of the Great Mosque or the blinding white marble of the dainty Moti Masjid; one might take him day after day to temples and halls of audience, and baths; there are crumbling memorials of the Mutiny for him to see; Hindu Rao's house, the Kashmir gate beneath which some still salute dead Home and Salkeld as they pass, and the tree-encumbered sites of redoubt and battery; for those who pick the worm-holes of long-vanished days there is Asoka's pillar; there is the already over-grown site of the great Durbar, for those whose interests are of to-day. But among all these things two stand out significant. One of them is the Diwan-i-khas, or private throne-room, of the palace in the fort.

It is an open hall, supported on a double row of many-cusped arches, daintily gilded here and there, and of heavy square columns, panelled and inlaid, of marble, here white, here ivory, there old gold in tint. One could swear that this forest of marble is translucent. The gilding upon it here and there stands forward and rejects the light that sinks softly into the onyx-like stone, upon which it is laid. And the inlaid flowers, whereof every leaf is jade and malachite, every petal is agate and lapis lazuli, so stand out upon this pearly bed that you might vow you could put your fingers behind the stalk and snap it. You will not at first understand the beauty and splendid restraint of the Diwan-i-khas; if you try four afternoons to sketch you may begin to realise that Austin de Bordeaux, a dishonest and fugitive jeweller from France, may yet prove to have been the first decorator of all known periods—decorator, not artist, nor perhaps architect, the point is in dispute. Quiet, restrained, his riot of colour spreads over these jewelled walls unfailing in taste, and perfect to the veining of a poppy-leaf or the stamen of one of those Crown Imperial lilies or blue-purple irises which his craftsmen never looked upon, though at the bidding of this immoral genius they faithfully translated into stone the humbled pride of the one and the cool transparency of the other. Everywhere the design is both natural and conventional, and the harmony of this vast and transcendent casket for the Peacock Throne deserves the famous Persian inscription, "If heaven be anywhere on earth, it is here, it is here, it is here." Outside there is hot sunshine, the blaze of a scarlet hybiscus across the lawn, and the soft and stealing scent of jasmine and orange-blossom.

The Peacock Throne—of which Lord Curzon has disinterred in the treasure-house of Teheran a noble fragment far finer than the Takt-i-taus which is generally shown to visitors as part of the spoils of Nadir Shah—was of gold. But the gold was scarcely visible for the rubies, diamonds, and sapphires, close set from end to end of the long low seat. A peacock "in his pride" stood behind at either end, and formed between them the greater part of the back. These two were of precious stones, only, I think, larger than those used in the seat. Also a parrot ensigned the centre of the back of the throne—the bird was cut from one single emerald. These statements appear to be the plain truth about the most magnificent jewel ever made on earth. They would be incredible had not, luckily, a French professional jeweller seen the throne before it was stolen by Nadir Shah in 1739 and partly broken up. Tavernier has left not only a description of the gorgeous thing, but an expert's estimate of its value—about £12,037,500 sterling, if expressed in to-day's currency. We have the casket of this jewel in the Diwan-i-khas, and it is worthy of that royal seat, even if the latter's beauty was equal to its cost. And in the Diwan-i-khas we have also the keynote and coping-stone of the policy of the Mogul dynasty of India.

But there is another thing to be seen in Delhi.

A corner of the Diwan-i-khas.

[*Facing page* 56.

Outside the battered Kashmir gate, whereto leans the plain stone which commemorates Home and Salkeld, is a stretch of uneven grass cut into by a diverging road. Across that, a little rise takes one through the cemetery gates, adjoining the squat lodge of the keeper, up to a railed-off tomb underneath a neem-tree. Inside there is a flat stone, with these words upon it: "The grave of Brigadier General John Nicholson, who led the assault of Delhi, but fell in the hour of victory, mortally wounded; and died 23rd September, 1857: aged 35." There have been many lives worth living in the last hundred years, but few indeed are fit to set beside John Nicholson's. There have been many deaths worth dying, but surely none since Nelson's that compares with his. Two men in two centuries regained India for us at the eleventh hour as she was slipping from our very fingers' ends. One—Clive—has long been forgotten; in all the length of this statue-laden country there is not a bust or a tablet to him. Twopenny-ha'penny administrators, banded about with ribands, have had their brazen tributes in every corner of India, while Clive, perhaps because he took his own life, still awaits his recognition. For his memorial, when it shall come, one is tempted to suggest " circumspice " once again as the only but sufficient record of his work. Of John Nicholson it can hardly be said that he has been forgotten, for in England he has never been recognised at all, while, on the other hand, out here in India the money for the statue that is even now being raised at Delhi in his honour, has come from such a variety of admirers that one is reminded of the austere administrator's popularity while he lived even among the very tribes whose women scared their children into quietness with the mere name of " Jan Nikasain." For English rule in India John Nicholson stands just as the gold and emeralds and marble of the Diwan-i-khas stand for the Mogul and his ideals.

But if there still survive a spirit of that dead and splendid dynasty, it does but breathe in the night wind that stirs the dead grasses along the Campagna of bygone Delhi, while Nicholson's ghost walks visibly abroad wherever sound and unselfish work is done by the lowest sahib-servant of this huge and helpless people entrusted to our care.

Lahore.

FRESH gardens and heavy trees beside well-kept roads, cool houses, and an upstanding English cathedral, dispersed over four square miles of ground, and beside the Mall the bitter smell and silence of a tan gallop. Offices there are, too, for the Punjab Government, roomy, and adequate; hospitals and colleges, institutes and horticultural gardens—all that makes for contentment and efficiency in Anglo-Indian life, gathered loosely over the flat between the curbed Ravi and the curving parallels of the great Bari Doab Canal. Thrust tightly into one upper corner of this city of distances and spaces, and nudging it uncertainly in half a dozen places, are the crooked elbows of the densely-packed native town. Beyond that, again, overlooking the wooded level to the north, an inhospitable bulk of red sandstone rises, sign unmistakable of yet another of the palace fortresses of the Moguls—this is Lahore.

In Lahore Akbar's shrewd judgment selected a green oasis among the then unfertile lands of the five rivers, and to him much of all the imperial magnificence of the city and palace is due. Yet, truth to tell, it comes to most travellers too late in their path. Agra and Delhi have come before it, and there is nothing in all the place to equal the dreamy perfection of the one or the costly splendour of the other. Only Akbar's huge gateway, with its encaustic tiles, strikes a note of originality, and the idle dreamer might spend an afternoon in piecing together from this strange and inconsequent series of figures of beasts and flowers and men and angels some key to that most elusive of all Oriental characters, Akbar himself. It is commonly said that one of the strait, stiff figures on the walls is no other than that of the Virgin Mary herself, and the suggestion is likely enough. Certainly Akbar's acquaintance with the Christianity of the Portuguese missionaries of Goa is proved. It is also clear that the priests were allowed some access to Murad and Jehangir,* his sons, and his Hall of Universal Worship at Fatehpur Sikri was almost American in its catholic tolerance. But it is difficult

* Upon the walls also of Jehangir's adjoining palace Bernier says that an image of the Virgin was set up, but it is impossible to trace it now.

AHMEDABAD

to disentangle fact and fiction in Oriental history as soon as religion is brought into the dispute. Indeed, the well-known legend that Akbar had a Christian wife—one Maria, a Portuguese maiden from Goa—seems to rest on the prejudiced interpretations of the missionaries of a later generation. Still, the man remains one of the enigmas of history, and in this hotch-potch of ornament it is a pleasant fancy that he may have had the whim to symbolise to himself his own infinitely varied interests, sympathies, and perhaps, if one had the clue, one might trace some of the vicissitudes also of his strange career.

But the thread of personal self-confidence runs all through his life. He asked no man to do what he would not, and could not, do himself. He once relieved Ahmedabad with a not inconsiderable force of cavalry, and kept up the speed of eighty miles a day. On another occasion he outrode completely the Ghent to Aix legend by reaching Ajmere from Agra, a distance of two hundred and twenty miles, in forty-eight hours. This he did for his own exercise and amusement, afterwards repeating the pilgrimage on foot in order to obtain a son and heir. In quiet days, lest he should wax rusty and luxurious, he executed a Domesday Book of his territories. His income was £52,000,000 a year, all of which was available for his ambitions. Consider his action at Fatehpur Sikri. To be with his teacher, the Sheikh Chisti, he builds a vast new palace-fort, new temples, and a new town round the hermit's lonely cell. He invites the learned of all religions to argue and dispute in his presence, and then, in the midst of this new prosperity, at a word of complaint from his religious friend about the noise that his city brought round his sequestered cell, gave orders, and Fatehpur Sikri became again as Nineveh, save that the clean chisel-marks may yet be seen upon the palace jambs and cornices. Certainly a man of decision and self-reliance.

There is a certain suitability in remembering the theological experiments of Akbar in this his capital of Lahore. For to-day also here is the centre of religious activity in the northern half of India, and even a slight acquaintance with the town must convince a visitor that if only for this reason the atmosphere of Lahore is, and must remain, different from that of other places. This is not the time or place to awaken the ever-vexed question of the success or failure of missionary effort among the races and castes of Hindustan. But it should

Kim on Zam-Zammah.

[*Facing page* 62.

in fairness be remembered that Lahore offers the best example of such work—work that, to its everlasting honour, concerns itself almost as mightily with the bodies as with the souls of the natives, whose confidence and gratitude have long been won. Akbar himself, it is to be borne in mind, was the founder of a religion which seems to have been a worship of Brahma or God the Creator, so basic and bold as to have been stripped of all but the enunciation of this one aboriginal article of faith. Upon this austere framework he then permitted all other sects to weave at will the distinguishing creeds and dogmas of their choice. It was thus unnecessary and, indeed, difficult to exclude from this over-universal church any faith that cared to emphasise its somewhat postulated belief in a First Cause. Perhaps for that very reason, because there was so little with which to disagree, so little about which to suffer martyrdom, Akbar's great scheme was doomed to failure, dying for sheer want of opposition. But as a bold attempt on the part of the greatest reformer, administrator, and despot of India, it has hardly received the attention that it deserves, especially at this moment, when education and religion seem likely to come to a compromise upon a highest common factor not wholly different from that which underlay the faith of Akbar.

In his large industry, capricious energy, autocratic methods, and confidence that he was in the personal confidence of God, the Emperor has his parallel in Germany to-day. Flaring upon the western pier of the gigantic gateway of the mosque at Fatehpur Sikri is the saying of Jesus Christ of Nazareth: "This world is as a bridge. Pass on, there is no tarrying here." Yet Akbar was far from being untouched by worldly pomps, as his slightest building testifies, and one is inclined to believe that he was well aware of the ambiguity of the war-cry of his new faith. "Allahu-Akbar" means either that God is great or that Akbar is God, and neither meaning was probably ever absent from his mind; nay, on one grim occasion, he felt the blasphemy, and retreated in confusion from the pulpit whence he was intoning his own creed.

In old days, before the creation of the North-West Frontier province, great was the pride of the Punjab; great in its own estimation was Lahore. There has been a fall, and the rest of the peninsula shows little sympathy with this much and deservedly lauded home of municipal administration. Its "C. and M. Gazette"—foster sister to the fine old "Pioneer"—has done its best, but the old glory is departed. There are many who regret the manner of her deposition: the act was inevitable. The truth is that its interests have become provincial rather than national, and that, as in the case of Madras, has sounded the death-knell of its old half-romantic attractiveness. Its frontier importance was the framework of its old pretensions, and now that that has been taken away there is as little and as much to fill out the garments of her past greatness as there is in the case of Madras. The administrative work is done equally well in both provinces. Indeed, for administrative models, India now turns rather to Madras than to Lahore, for in the jealous eyes of other districts, even this supremacy is departing from the northern city. But Lahore still holds a high head. All India smiled a year or two ago. An inscription had to be framed for the memorial to William Brendish, the telegraph clerk, whose fidelity to his post while Delhi roared and murdered in the streets without needs no retelling here "The electric telegraph saved India." Montgomery's verdict is on the record, but the good folk of Lahore put on the memorial this artless ascription of credit, that Brendish had "rendered invaluable service to the Punjab Government." To this day few in Lahore outside the office of the "Civil and Military" have seen the humour of this.

For the rest, Lahore and its picturesque variety of construction, material, and style is like enough to any other North Indian city, like in the crowded sea of humanity in her streets, like in the passing interest evoked by the shrine of a saint, the tomb of a courtier, or one of those random mosques that so often took the place of conscience-money in the East, like in the dainty legends of love or hate, of the favour of a king, or the jealousy of a woman, that mesh in every gathering of human habitations in royal India. Ranjit Singh is buried here, and with him the eleven Court ladies who passed alive through the fiery gate with his dead body. The armoury distinguishes the fort from others, and a trace of especial interest attaches to the French accoutrements which tells a tale of long-vanished ambitions. Here, also, is the identical sword with which the first great Guru founded the Sikh religion. The latter may also, I believe, be seen in the treasury of the Golden Temple at Amritsar.

I have kept to the last the central interest of Lahore. The museum treasures, among which the

Lama of Such-zen discussed the Way with the white-bearded Englishman, remain for the antiquarian, the traveller, and the historian one of the fascinating enigmas of India. They are now housed in a new and spacious building, and all down the long gallery and on either side the close-set relics stand side by side. Strange memorials are they of the day when two empires, Buddhism and Hellenism, met and mingled where three empires now meet but never mingle—nay, they draw, instead, painfully exact lines of division and dislike. Greek in all but name, these full-rounded faces and royally posed heads surmount drapery such as India could never hang. It is a tale that has not yet been told in full, this slow reception of the exiles of a defeated and expelled faith, by frontiersmen, exiles themselves, in whom no luxury or pride had betrayed the tradition of Pheidias and his school. Nowhere in the world is Buddhism portrayed so finely as in these stones. For the essential and tranquil quietism of the Master's creed lost nothing and gained humanity in the hands of men whose forefathers carved the Venus of Milo or the Demeter of the British Museum. Both exiles and hosts among these Himalayan barriers of the north had relearned in hard life and forced renunciation some portion of those primitive truths that were so quickly swamped in the laziness and easy living of the plains from which each had originally come.

Nor is this all their interest for us. These blackened, sharply-cut stones, still showing chisel marks, if you look for them, are all, or nearly all, that is left of Buddhism in India, in the land of its birth; all, at least, that can connectedly, and with wealth of example, retell the story of the Light of Asia scene by scene and triumph by triumph. These carvings have been collected by many hands along the frontier. They were rescued from the neglect of those who follow a creed different indeed from that of the Master, and it is well that they are gathered here together, for even now, many years after the discovery of most of the statues, a scholar would have to take his life in his hand were he to re-visit the hill-villages from which they came. There are still many places teeming with Græco-Buddhist treasures, but the Lahore collection is so rich, indeed so sated with duplicates, that one may almost regard this collection as complete for most necessary purposes. And we owe it all to that white-bearded Englishman, no other than Mr. Lockwood Kipling, that we have these treasures safely housed in Lahore. For it is a mistake to suppose that Indian officials, even to-day, care much for the archæology of their district. There are exceptions, of course, Lord Curzon, while viceroy, being himself the chief, but, in old days, it needed strength and courage, as well as knowledge and taste, to foster the unique collection which, when all is said and done, remains the real treasure of the capital of the province of the Five Great Rivers of Hindustan. Nay, these half prehistoric relics will be of scant interest to many travellers as well. So let them take garries and drive six miles out to the marble pavilions and exquisitely confined waters of the Shalimar Gardens.

The Khyber.

For one thousand five hundred miles from its source on the right bank of the Hugli, thirty miles north of Calcutta, the Grand Trunk Road unfolds its thin, shadow-flecked ribbon of white metal across the heart of India. By Gaya, Benares, Delhi, Amritsar, and Lahore, on to the gates of far-distant Peshawar, beyond the ken of the farthest surveyor of the engineers of Aurangzeb, the track strikes fairly across the densest populations of the peninsula. Nay, on through the pass itself it is but the Grand Trunk Road that has been carried on yet another stage. A hundred yards beyond the fort of Landi Kotal, the Khyber witnesses the extinction of the most historic highway of the East, and up to the last rod of it the great trail is worthy of its reputation.

It was well enough said the other day that nothing, however important, in the internal administration of India can ever hope to rival in interest the frontier questions—those eternal prob-

The Shalimar Gardens, Lahore.

The End of the Grand Trunk Road, beyond Landi Kotal.

[*Facing page* 70.

lems symbolised by the golden roofs of Lhasa and the grim defiles of the Khyber. It is all the less accountable, therefore, that there hardly exists, for anyone who has not actually visited the spot, any very clear idea of the famous cleft in the Himalayas through which the thin trickle of merchandise ebbs and flows between India and the North, and on which so many years of hard military work and close political thought have been concentrated. India—the remark is a platitude—so far as the passage of large bodies of troops is concerned, is an island except for this scanty line of communication, and upon the safe keeping of the Khyber and its auxiliaries, most of the Indian military strategy of fifty years has been pivoted.

Out from Peshawar one goes along the hard, grey, enamelled track, past the gardens and trees of the cantonment, which appears to be peaceful, even beyond the ordinary stagnation of these deceptive enclaves of military control. Nothing could prepare one less for what is to come than the luxurious growth of close-grown tolly, umbrageous banyan, and dusty-spined casuarina, overhanging the low white-washed walls that divide the compounds and the coarsely-grassed lawns from the roadway. Grass is the trouble of Indian gardens. There is a stretch or two at Calcutta and at Agra ; lawns are encouraged to continue to live round Akbar's tomb and the Taj, but it is all rather a pretence, and Lord Kitchener, at the Pindi manœuvres last year, boldly faced the fact that turf—as opposed to grass—is an exotic, and bought instead twenty hundredweight of mustard and cress seed to make the little plot of his great encampment green and soft underfoot. It was rumoured that had there been another maund in India he would have bought it also.

Every now and then the square, low walls of a barrack can be seen through the trees, and the last examining station is passed close beside the police lines on the south side of the road. It is neither of interest nor importance in itself, but close on the post the scene changes with a suddenness that is unmistakable. Man has combined with Nature to put a sudden end here to the greenery and the groves of polyglot Peshawar. Man demanded a clear glacis of a mile for his riflemen, uncovered, flat, and from end to end capable of being commanded and swept by those innocent-looking, khaki-tinted mud-walls ; but even before the farthest edge of this mile was reached, Nature had given up its brave struggle with the increasing aridity and the uncompromising stoniness of the last up-wash of India against the Himalayan barrier. Henceforth it is a rocky and treeless waste. The road still strikes westwards, level, straight, and smooth. On either side the coarse sand of the plain stretches away, rarely furrowed here and there by dry watercourses, nourishing here and there an even rarer patch of tilth. It is used occasionally as a divisional parade ground, though, for the most part of the year, it lies out as empty as the sea.

To right and left the mountain spurs have thrust themselves forward to meet one on either side, but the gullet of the Khyber is not reached for some six or seven miles yet, so deeply into the hills does this tongue of Indian sand penetrate. To right and left the long promontories of grey gault, clad only with spotted bushes of stunted wild olive, advance spies of their gigantic brethren whose blue outlines blend into the sky, mount upwards from the plain till they are capped and pinnacled or overborne by the heavy walls of Himalayan gneiss and granite. In the middle of this deep recess stands up Jamrud, yellow in the sun, blue purple in the shade, a fine, upstanding fort of mud and stone, embattled and bastioned like the fortress of a fairy tale, and perhaps almost as useless against modern weapons. Just as the flag on the keep's summit can be distinguished, India stops beneath one's feet.

Here is the frontier; beyond is no man's land. Ours, indeed, it is, by the right of the nine points of the law, and by the necessity of the case, but part of India it is not. Three miles short of Jamrud the turmoils and the administrative problems, the constitutional rights and duties, the dust and thrust of our Imperial altruism fall behind, and we come out into the real arena to face the elemental facts of life. Here self-preservation is the only law that sanctions, and the game is played with vigour, and with something of the law of the jungle besides. Jamrud and the Khyber do not exist for the delectation of idle men. It is true that on occasions when it may be convenient, when, that is, the pass is guarded, and its peaceful transit guaranteed for some other purpose than that of curiosity, for such a purpose as the passage of the bi-weekly caravan from Kabul, then, and only then, may the idler have leave to drive out to see the entering in of the famous defile. He will enjoy it the more because of his fearful and delightful belief that he takes his life in his hand, and that behind each rock may lurk the jezail and hairy ruffian of his long expectation. As a matter of fact, he will but be rudely treated by camels and will suffer much dust. His life will be safer far in the pass than when in a hired fly he went yesterday down into Peshawar bazaar from the hotel to buy a handful of turquoises from a fat Parsee merchant lolling over his accounts, or a Penjdeh rug in the foul donkey market, where among the mud and dung and flies the real treasures are unwillingly spread out to those who understand—blinking "elephant-foot" sun-traps of maroon and crimson, and creamy white, bound about with white and black yak-hair ropes, or Khirgah purdahs with "snuff" terminals, glowing with the purples and greens of a pheasant's neck. Europeans are not wanted here. Gregson is allowed in always, and Colonel Hendley might even be welcomed as one initiated, but these glories of Central Asian work, each the work of seven or, maybe, seventeen years, are marked down by such men as Ghulam Mahommed "the lame," or Ghulam Rasul, merchants of Rawal Pindi. Englishmen do not understand their value yet. But if you go and buy them in Peshawar you *may* get in the way of a ghazi—a poor devil earning Paradise at your expense. If you keep to the road in the Khyber you are safer than at many a London crossing.

From Jamrud the road still runs on the flat across a wide, torrent-seamed bed of rock and sand, up to the very tip of the tongue of land. Here the ascent begins between rough boulder-strewn slopes; these soon give way to steep acclivities and shoulders of bare rock, round which the road sweeps and recurs in an easy and ever-ascending gradient. The Shadi-bagiari blockhouse commands the entrance to the pass, and Fort Maude follows soon, just where the old plastered bridge between the wild mulberry and the tolly tree imports a breath of greenery and civilisation into the rocky wilderness between the bare blasted-out road at one's feet and the forbidding grassless skyline far overhead. Still ascending, the road skirts Shahgai and the little cultivation plots of Lala-china a mile or two before the tiny high-perched group of blockhouses known as Ali Masjid. The name is taken from a blindingly whitewashed little shrine that marks a grave in a little plot a few feet above the little stream. The Khyber rivulet flashes by, muttering between its pebbles, and sadly dwindled by the irrigation canal that runs sedately beside it, closely hugging the contours of the rock.

On the opposite side rises the sharp conical promontory or group of promontories which guards the gorge itself. For here—and here alone, throughout the pass's length till Landi Kotal is reached—there is a steep rock-bound defile, out of which the road is cut on the north-eastern side, and by which all further view of the Khyber is entirely shut out. This sense of privacy is emphasised by the road sentries a hundred yards further on. No one, except those who are accompanied by a "Khyber Rifle" as an escort, is allowed to pass this barrier, and the escort is only granted for special reasons. Bribery, blarney, or bluff, all are useless here, and it is as well that you should not try to steal through. Neither English nor Hindustani do the warders understand, but their orders they most entirely do, and a German who tried to force his way through, the other day, was significantly congratulated on the failure of his attempt. For here is business, real business—short shrifts are given, and few excuses are accepted.

The blockhouses of the Khyber are models of their kind, and the very sight of their shrewdly-pierced loopholes, their machicoulis galleries, and their first-floor entrances and hanging ladders, will impress you long before you notice that at your elbow, on the rock beside you, is a careless splash of whitewash—five hundred yards range this one, and across the valley a deftly-placed series from three hundred to one thousand—a splash which one day it will be sheer suicide to approach. Still climbing, the road now follows the course of the tinkling stream, now strikes across the bottom of a tiny flat pan of ploughland, just where, beside the road, ill-shapen masses of wood are being weighed. They have been brought in by women from the hills, and to-morrow will have started down to Peshawur, which takes every stick of firewood that the pass can provide. From one point of view, this stripping of the pass has its advantages—for even as late as forty years ago the hillsides were thickly-wooded enough to afford considerable cover—but the loss of the vegetation affects, and is in turns affected by, the rainfall, to an extent which is annually becoming more and more unmistakable. Gnarled and stunted wild olives, two or three species of thorn, rarely a rowan tree—still more rarely upon the higher slopes to the north, a small oak which is known locally as a totarra—these make up the robuster vegetation of the valley.

Major Roos Keppel, the presiding deity of the

pass, enforces law and order in a quaint and effective way. In the rights and wrongs of tribal disputes he will not enter. Only one thing is sacred—the Road. On that road no man shall be killed. Twenty yards to right and left is the hunting-ground of the Khels, and Keppel is not there to meddle. But woe betide the village within whose district a road-murder occurs.

So this little strip of civilisation runs on, beset on either side with the manners and customs of Troglodytes armed with magazine rifles. At Katakushta we pass from the territory of the Malik-dins to that of the Wali Khels, and we enter the Khyber proper. This name is given by the Khels to a comparatively small and insignificant part of the pass. A Kuki Khel from Shadi-bagiari and a Zakka Khel from Landi Kotal will speak alike of making a journey to the Khyber; Ali Masjid itself is regarded as being outside the limits, and the adoption of the name by ourselves for the entire pass is due chiefly, of course, to the convenience of having some inclusive name, but partly also to the fact that in this part of the gorge, near Zin-tarra, there is the one and only remarkable monument of its entire length. This is a large and originally a well-built Buddhist tope. An Indian tope is a plain structure dating in almost every case from a comparatively early period—being, of course, in date anterior to, or contemporary with, the expulsion of the Buddhists from India in the seventh and eighth centuries; this, as perhaps making a refuge to which the expelled Buddhists escaped, may be somewhat later,—consisting of a platform surmounted by a plain dome. Much of the exterior casing of the Zin-tarra tope has been pulled down for building material, but it preserves its shape, and in one less accessible part it still keeps its closely-fitted exterior masonry. The dome must originally have been about as large as that of the Invalides, and the square platform below projects well beyond the drum.

Beyond the tope and the twin villages of the Sultan Khels and the Niklei Khels, the road lifts to the watershed plateau, where the long low blank walls of Landi Kotal command a hundred acres of fairly level ground. Landi Kotal is not built for beauty, but inside its fortifications is a pleasant little garden, where there is a well overrun with purple convolvulus and zinnias, and rambling roses prepare one for the few stout shafts of English hollyhock which bloom sturdily enough in this Ultima Thule of Britain. Nor is this all that

A Kafila in the Khyber Pass.

[*Facing page* 80.

reminds one of home. Inside the mess of the Khyber Rifles, there, on the wall in front of you, is a series of "Spy's" portraits and—an engraving of the "Beata Beatrix"! Yet one is really in the uttermost of all outposts, and the precautions of a post in the enemy's country are stringently observed by day and by night.

One can still walk three or four miles on, beyond the friendly levels of the Grand Trunk Road, over a rough camel track and cart road, to a lonely post called Mishnai Khandao, perched on the edge of a precipitous rock. From here, Pisgah-like, you may dangle your legs over, and look down upon the "Black Stones" and the interlocking spurs of the pass to the flat brown plain and the far white minarets of an Afghan tomb beside the Kabul river.

Through the sunset we went back to Landi Kotal, passing through the large walled compound, where the Kafila or Kabul caravan was resting for the night. Great shaggy-throated and black-headed camels, half as tall again as those of India, loomed out of the obscurity, and tiny groups of incurious women and lazy men gathered round the gipsy fires, at which the evening meal was being cooked. Half-round each party lay a rampart of the heavy corded bundles they were bringing into India. Out-

6

side the wall of the compound one could see a dozen heads rise and fall together in outline against the darkening sky as the last prayer of the day was said and the last prostration made to the red west that curtained distant Mecca. Almost in the dark we went back past the three water-tanks, stumbling up against a placid Shinwari, who, for an expected gain of a few pice, was trudging along to distant Peshawar beside his pony, laden with dirty snow from the winter pits of Mallagori.

Agra.

The waters of the holy Jumna, descending idly to her even holier sister-stream, fetch a wide half-circle through their ever-shifting "javeaux" and the firm, flat, sandy islets where the city's washing makes gay mosaic in the morning sun. Agra crowds down to the water's edge along the outer curve. In flood time the opaque green waters, as they sweep round from north-east to north-east again, lap nearly up to the stark walls of the Mogul fort, which stands out from afar, the crimson heart of the dun, dull, dome-spotted native city. In the early dawn the skeins of river mist sway, like white gauze, all round the great curve, and just before they float upwards and are dissipated they catch the amethyst of the false sunrise that precedes the up-leap of the strong Indian sun across the low, empty levels of the eastern bank. Beyond the fort the houses retreat from the river's margin, and a space of tangled scrub and low jungle dips to the sandy waste through which the Jumna picks her way. A mile and a half down stream, among her own forest trees and high on her own marble river-wall, rises the Taj.

The last resting-place of Shah Jehan and the woman he loved is for many travellers, perhaps for all, the crown and goal of all that India has of beauty and romance. Generations have come and gone since that far day when the most splendid of all earth's emperors bowed his head to the dust before his darling's tiny little coffin in the vault of the finished Taj, all new and white and glistening. There has hardly been a traveller in all that time who, in his own way, sage or sentimental, has not tried to set down his estimate of this marvel in stone. Some have found safety in mere suggestion and a reverent withdrawal from the task; others have laid their measuring chains along its courses from plinth to crescent finial, vainly seeking in exact computation the secret that died in the very lifetime of the architect, died with the occasion that called forth the Taj. Yet for all their pains, for all that the building is better known than any other in the world, there may still be room for a plain description of the tomb of Arjumand, the Exalted of the Palace. Photography has done its best, but it is possible that nothing has ever baffled the lens so elusively as these white marbles; certainly no man who ever came to understand them has once looked at his photograph of them without a puzzling sense of disappointment. It was a living woman with the breath of life between her lips of whom he made his sun-picture; beneath the dull ruby of his dark room the film gives back the features of the dead.

There is one matter I should like to make clear. Unwise admirers of the Taj have done her even more injustice than the camera. It is absurd to deny the professional architect his scope and privilege. There are defects, even grave defects, in the design, which sentimental souls are foolish to deny. They will not see that the fact that the expert is right in his criticisms does not make them wrong. It is inevitable that this antagonism should arise. Mechanical perfection has ever been a foe to a deeper lying charm. Salisbury Cathedral from end to end is perfect. There is no tampering with the clean-run homogeneity of the pile. The thirteenth century, the era beyond all others of English Gothic, bestowed its ripened genius upon the Minster of the Plain, and the church as it is to-day is that from which the loosened scaffolding fell away six centuries ago. But is it not common knowledge that Salisbury, from its very perfection, leaves the visitor dissatisfied and chilled. Man is not fit for such inhuman certainty, such skill infallible.

The plate here given is a picture of a sweeper sweeping in a garden. It is true that the Taj makes his background, but that is how one should look at it. It is an old trick, well enough known to artists, but never more certain of its effect than here. The colour of the Taj, its mystery, its lightness and its strength, are tenfold more to be understood when the eye does not directly challenge its beauty. The man who stands on the central marble cistern and makes his photograph deserves the failure which awaits him.

Here at Agra the architectural excellence is not too wholly perfect for our poor human nature. Let us accept the artist's condemnation of the black marble "pointing" between the white stones of the minarets; let us admit that the minarets themselves were an experiment of doubtful success; from the architect let the charge that the tomb is "all gateway" remain, if not exactly accepted, at any rate unanswered; nay, one may even admit that from the standpoint of northern tastes there is a regrettable sameness about the view from the four points of the compass. These are perfectly justifiable and even interesting comments, and it is silly to object to them. Perhaps Ustad Isa—or was it Verroneo or Austin de Bordeaux?—would have made alterations himself if he had had the work to do again, just as Ictinos confessed at Phigaleia for all the world to see the strange mistake he made in the matter of the frieze of the Parthenon. What, after all, do these mistakes matter, save that they bring the warm humanity of the Taj, its most intimate claim upon our love, a little nearer and a little dearer still into our hearts. Nay more, for all that distinguishes mankind from brutes on the one hand and successful business operators on the other, the Taj is touchstone supreme. You have but to pass through the red sandstone gateway, and look along the water garden to the place itself, and your first comment will tell us more about yourself than about the world-famous tomb.

In the central cistern cool lotuses spread themselves in plates of bronze and green at the water-level—a resting place for diamond-winged dragon flies, of scarlet or olivine; beside them the wet rods of flowering rush spring up in a dainty faggot, tied where reality and reflection meet. A faint ripple of moving water throws a tangle of light upon the marble edge of conduits, that lead the eye continually between the jasmine and orange and all the scented undergrowth of an Indian garden, up to the haven where it would rest, and the dreamy translucence of the vast building floats in sunny silence, pearl-white against the pale ultramarine of the lower sky.

If you look you will see between the trees a panel-sided platform of marble. It is twenty feet high, but it looks scarcely ten. Every side of it is a hundred yards long, but you will have to pace the distances to believe it. Upon the plinth the Taj itself rises, silver in the light and turquoise blue in the shadows. A great gateway lifts itself clear—too clear, alas!—for the avenue of black-green cypress flambeaux is gone, and our grand-children alone may hope to see again this subtle and splendid glory of the gardens. On either side is a double-storeyed flank, so deeply recessed that its lines of pure marble seem less the main construction of the building than the white meshes of the rich blue mysteries of the eight arched openings that attend the gate. Above, two clean

THE TAJ.

lotus-pointed cupolas rise, humble ministers to the swelling purity of the great white dome, which crowns and recomposes all into harmony and peace.

At each corner of the platform a tall minaret stands sentinel about the place where Mumtaz sleeps. On either side, across the marble court-yards on the right hand and on the left, the red guardian "Question and Answer" mosques face inwards to the Taj. Careless they are of facing east or west. The ritual of Islam bows before the stress of human love, and through the solemn spaces of the tomb, to the dead ears of the Emperor and his love, they cry aloud in eternal antiphon the greatness and the majesty of God. Beyond on the north, the Jumna circles past the white abutments, and all round rises the green foliage of trees and the heavy scent of jasmine and roses.

Inside, in the gathered darkness behind the impenetrable walls of marble, barely relieved by their heavy latticed windows, a musical silence hovers beneath the dim vault whereunder the exquisite screen still guards the twin cenotaphs. The bodies of the lovers lie in the crypt below. In the obscurity one may well miss the quiet loveliness of this perforated and jewelled screen; yet Austin de Bordeaux, thief and fugitive though he was, scamped never a leaf-veining or a chisel-touch as he inset grey purple spar beside a whorl of cream onyx, or sparingly laid a touch of raw emerald just where the green-ribbed agates of the fillet turn in their milky bed of Jaipur alabaster. And all this labour and love was bestowed where, so far as Austin could ever guess, only the occasional smoky glare of a red torch would ever reveal its beauties for a passing moment.

Other buildings in the world have their own personal identity, their own attitude towards the ways and loves of men. St. Mark's challenges the inner lives of men, St. Peter's the crooking of their knees, the Pyramids confront the rising and the setting sun, the polestar and all the celestial company, Salisbury gazes coldly and very certainly upwards into heaven. The Taj Mahal alone crouches together, still huddled in loveliness and utter misery, crying only to be left alone with her dead. There is no front to the Taj; go where you will, she turns away, and will have none of the world's consolation, its sympathy, or, worst of all, its admiration. Blind with her own tears.

she dwells apart, the spirit of love incarnate, realising to the bitter dregs the uselessness of raising jewelled homes of marble for the unresponsive dead. Arjumand is dead, is dead, and not all the wealth of him who never had an earthly rival in splendour can buy back one fleeting hour. It is misery made manifest.

You will understand the Taj best if you will wait till the rosy fleeces have faded in the afterglow and the ripples of the Jumna run steel-grey in the waning light. A bird springs up, and the leaves of the thuia and the pepal murmur together as the darkness grows. A flying-fox with leathern wings wheels down from above, and a morrice of bats heralds the coming of the moon in the utter silence. And then you will understand that it does not matter whether you can still see the Taj or not. It is no question now of dome or gateway, silver work, or inlaid jewels. But as the dusk deepens you will come to know that the frail little body buried far down in its jewelled alabaster beside her faithful lord stands, and must always stand, for all that men hold dear or sacred in this world. However splendid and costly it may be, however renowned, however beautiful, the Taj itself is but an emblem and a symbol—so long as men and women love upon this earth, so long shall they go to the quiet garden beside the Jumna to lay their flowers in honour of Mumtaz alone, not of Ustad Isa, not of Shah Jehan, nor of another. For she loved and was much beloved.

Jammu.

It was a swelteringly hot noonday, and Jammu had proved somewhat barren of interest except as a panorama from the Prime Minister's unfinished Anglo - Hindu - Kashmiri palace - villa on Ramnagar. The museum—which had its origin as a spacious house run up so recently before the visit of the present Emperor in 1875 that he wisely decided not to risk sleeping in the still wet, plastered rooms—was suffering, like many other things in India, from an energetic spring-cleaning and rearrangement. So far only the necessary ordeal of dirt and a general state of locked-upness had been achieved, and the stag's-horn chandeliers of the verandah hardly repaid the trouble of the climb, though they had evidently impressed the khansamah of the noble guest-house which here condescends to act as a dak bungalow. The great temple was not without interest, and it was a source of mixed gratification to note that the costly compliment of a tomb with a gilded copper dome had been paid to the memory of shrewd old Golab Singh, who, in 1846, bought our interest in Jammu and Kashmir, lock, stock, and barrel, for half the price of a new hotel in Piccadilly.

Once upon a time there seemed a chance that in sheer desperation and poverty Kashmir would have to be taken over again by the Indian Government, but this last chance of regaining control was thrown away when one Walter Lawrence was sent by the Viceroy to set the financial system of the country upon a better footing. For the reforms he instituted—one of the soundest pieces of financial administration that India has known—not only set the twin States of Jammu and Kashmir on their legs again, but have resulted in such plethoric money-bags that the Maharaja's great brother, Sir Amar Singh, prime minister, commander-in-chief, and guardian tutelary of the territories, hardly knows how to spend the accumulated revenues. But he is wisely spending them on railways, which solves the difficulty of the surplus for himself—and will probably double it for his successor.

The palace is unimpressive—a large quadrangle with every side built in a different style. One is an erection, of no particular style, that sears the eye with its white-hot wash; a second suggests Venice; a third, departmental offices at Simla; and the fourth is frankly inspired by the Victoria railway station at Bombay. There is a curious custom symbolised by a wooden cage in an open structure in the market-place. Into this a new Maharaja enters, almost on his hands and knees, to receive the tilak, or caste mark, from a priest, as a necessary preliminary to his full recognition as head of the State. It is only just to say that this statement was denied *in toto* by one elderly inhabitant of Jammu. Like Fuller of old, "the Writer intricated leaveth all to the Last Day,"—a necessity that is more frequent in India than the glib narratives of many good writers and experienced "qui hais" would suggest. However, there the wooden cage is, and it seems ill-adapted for any other use.

The bazaar is indistinctive of anything. Babies, huge-cup-moulds of raw salt looking like pink sugar-candy; the usual crimson-bearded Mohammedans of a certain age, which they are anxious to dissemble, the usual pirate bulls nosing about among the sellers of vegetable stuffs, a few hill sheep, which always suggest that a paper-fastener must be used to keep in its strained position the huge, fat, upturned tail of pink and wool. Nothing was remarkable in all this. An officer of the Imperial Service troops and I wandered on, and then remembered a word of advice as we left the bungalow. Someone on an official visit to the State authorities shouted after us: "Go and see the tigers, if you have time." We asked where the cage of tigers was, and we went to it. We found a strangely interesting thing, something, indeed, that seemed better fitted to belong to a new Jungle Book than to the serious region of fact. Yet the story is exactly true. It was so curious that we took some pains to verify it.

We had been told that the Maharaja of Jammu possessed the finest male tiger kept in captivity anywhere in the world. This, I should say, is unquestionably true. Our informant might have added that his mate was the worst-tempered prisoner of any menagerie on earth. The cage in which these two are kept is a jerry-built erection of bricks and plaster. The iron bars are as thick as a little finger, and are inserted in the mortar between the bricks at the top. A good deal of the mortar has fallen, and, thanks to the anger of the lady inside, some more of it fell while we were

Jammu.

[*Facing page* 96.

looking on. It did not increase our sense of safety to notice that the bars do not reach to the bottom, but are held in place by two or three traverses of iron. The tiger, a glorious brute of white and orange and black, with steel sinews and teeth like Sikh daggers, lay sulkily in his cage and growled. The attendant was a man of whom some idea should be conceived. Five-foot four and thin, old and a little wasted in face, with a long, sparse beard of a hundred hairs stirring in the wind; his eyes sunken, but looking straight into your own, with heavy bistred circles low on his cheek-bones, his puggary of white gauze falling deep on either side below his ears, and his almost toothless mouth stained with red catechu—he made up an *ensemble* that was still dignified, a man to the marrow. Indeed, he let us know that he was of the lordly race of Nadaun, long exiled from the Punjab, and forced to adopt the faith of Islam. As he spoke the tigress again and again flung herself furiously against the flimsy bars; white people maddened her especially it seemed. Her lord growled steadily, and drew in his breath with a bubbling sound. The keeper put his anatomy of a hand under his kothi and pulled out a little white bag.

7

Some years ago, Mangal—I suppose the pair had been trapped on a Tuesday—found that the little back-door of his den was open. The assistant of the little menagerie returned to find him loose in the garden, and fled incontinently. In half an hour Jammu's streets were as those of a dead city. One informant told us that the soldiers, especially, were on the roofs of the houses. Tired of inaction, Mangal stole out and glided silently down the main street of the town, a beautiful vision of orange and black striped death. No man hindered him, and he went down to the jungle beside the Tavi, and vanished. An hour afterwards the keeper came back to his work and heard the news. A few minutes later another solitary figure made its way down the still empty streets of Jammu, with bowed head, beneath the glare of the sun. He had no weapon. Only, as he said, he had put on a leather coat to keep Mangal from scratching him. It was a touch that made the incident flash up before the eyes so instantly and truly that from a European it must have seemed an unpardonable touch of artistic affectation. He had his little white bag in his hand, and he went quietly down the deserted ways and was lost to sight in the jungle. An hour later he returned bare-headed in the sun. At his heels,

Nadoun, keeper of the tigers, Jammu.

[*Facing page* 98.

fawning and kittenish, slouched Mangal, and round the tiger's neck was loosely tied one end of Nadaun's white puggary.

Will you try to reconstruct what the sight must have been? Up over the hard hot cobbles and mud of the empty streets moved the pair. Nadaun, unhesitating and even-paced, never looking back, or varying the steady exchange of his thin legs, beneath the gaze of the thousands thronging the flat roofs overhead, all in the utter silence of such excitement that the only sound heard was the mutter of the Tavi far in the valley below. Behind him, ludicrously leashed with the long, frail puggary, the silken-coated brute padded uncertainly with dripping mouth and bared teeth. It was the little white bag that had done it.

"Would your honours like to see the effect of this medicine?" Nadaun put his hand into the bag, and scattered a few whitish grains inside the bars. In a moment Mangal was upon them with a deep bass cough, and his great, rough, red tongue was searching out the tiniest scrap of whatever it was. In fifteen seconds he was yawning, and a slathering stream was dripping from his mouth. In thirty seconds he was on his back in the middle of the cell, wriggling from side to side, and beating the air with his huge paws, like a kitten played with by a child. Nadaun put his arm in and pulled his whiskers. Mangal smiled fatuously, and pretended to bite.

This is actually what happened. It is difficult to explain the reason. Nadaun very naturally refused to allow us to look closely at the powder. It was his livelihood, he said, and his secret, if our honours would pardon him, must be kept. Probably valerian enters into the compound, but it is difficult to suggest any drug that could have so immediate a result. A few grains were given to the tigress also; the effect upon her was as much more striking, as she had been more furious but a minute before.

It was all very odd, and the main street took on a new interest as we went back past the long caravans of bullock carts, which were even then slowly carrying out the innumerable necessities and furniture destined for the camp at Satwari, which was to be used by the Prince of Wales during his brief stay at Jammu. What a camp that was! Electricity everywhere, and the humblest tent lined with Kashmiri embroideries and shawls. A stream had been deflected to make for beauty in the garden of the camp. Not for drinking, mark you;

it will scarcely be believed, but the very cows which provided milk for the camp had, for six weeks beforehand, been watered with boiled and filtered water, and the bathrooms were supplied with the same somewhat luxurious liquid.

As we returned, at the gate of the bungalow the guard of honour, provided for the Maharaja on the occasion of his state visit to the Resident, six-footers every man, swung past us to the skirl of the pipes, beneath their colours of crimson and gold, with Lakshmi dancing decorously in the middle.

Calcutta.

The last few hours of the journey from the west into Calcutta are as interesting as any that railway travel in India can give us. The low, flat, water-sodden delta of the Ganges stretches out to the horizon, but so great is the wealth of vegetation that twenty yards is often as far as one can see, except where some reedy bank, flaming with patches of rose lotus, opens out between the cocoa-nuts, teaks, and bananas that continually shut in the view with their half-translucent green curtain. Everything is rank in growth and rich in colour. In the early morning the mere telegraph wires are curves of hanging diamonds; the dripping morning dew has fringed every leaf with its own jewels, and the very sleepers of the railway flash with white fire as the sun strikes uncertainly between the foliage of the virgin jungle. Here and there an abandoned hut is almost hidden in the folds of the yellow karela upon its roof-tree, or of the up-

SUNRISE ON THE HUGLI.

springing pampas or datura beside its falling walls; here and there the jungle-overgrown house of some old Frenchman pretends that it is a human habitation still, and the crazy door-jambs and fungused lintels stand away under the bulging weight of their red bricks above. Chinsurah and Chandernagore are passed. For the former we exchanged Sumatra —no small price; the great pink palace, almost abutting on the railway station of the latter, has the picturesque but wholly unjust reputation of having been built as a haven of refuge by an absconding debtor from Calcutta, who found a permanent home among the easy-going Frenchmen in this fever-ridden place. As a matter of fact, there is little here of romance; the arm of the English is long, and the French do not care to have their scanty acres clogged with those who have left Calcutta for Calcutta's good. For on many days the reek of the long-drawn veil of smoke that always hems in their southern horizon can be smelled, so near is the metropolis of India.

The train comes into the Howrah terminus on the western bank of the Hugli, and the bridge, almost as famous and as cosmopolitan as that of Pera, has to be crossed. On the left is the sacred ghat, where devotees assembled to bathe before even Job Charnock, of questionable fame, came up from Madras hunting for leave to set up a factory and a few square acres on which to build it. Aurangzeb the Magnificent gave him a piece of land at Sutanati in 1690. The pleasant imaginings of writers have taken such hold that it is firmly believed in Calcutta that he landed at Boytakhana Bazar, and sat down under the pipal to ruminate upon the future greatness of this fever-ridden swamp. As a matter of fact, there were English already at Sutanati, which is the modern Rathtola Ghat, and Charnock's chief service to the State lay rather in his iron character than in his morals or in his foresight. For it is generally conceded now that Calcutta, built upon a stagnant swamp, painfully reclaimed from the crumbling alluvial drift of the Ganges, has attained her high position in despite of, rather than as a result of, any prophetic value attaching to this choice. For example, there is to-day a grave uncertainty whether the subsoil of the Maidan is able to support the Victoria Memorial Hall which is to be built in the middle of the large public park, in the heart of Calcutta. This will explain perhaps the enormous expense which has been incurred by seven generations of

A CALCUTTA SUNSET

men in turning "Sutanati" into the second city of the Empire.

Flat and well-metalled roadways of great width skirt by the maidan or dive through the many-storeyed buildings of Calcutta. Electric light and electric tramways put the richest parts of London to shame. Shops that are barely less in size and importance than their namesakes in England line the better-known streets, and houses encircled by well-tended gardens form suburbs that keep up the tradition of luxury that Hastings well understood and Macaulay accepted. If the buildings are not as eye-compelling as those of Bombay, it is only because the inhabitants have hesitated to accept the architecture with which the Western metropolis has unfortunately been content; they are no less commodious, and one day will be rebuilt with a permanence better deserved than that of the best Parsi-Gothic of Bombay.

Yet Calcutta is a dull town. It is flat and unlovely from end to end. There is never a corner to be turned in it which lets in a new scene. The bazaars are duller than any others in Hindustan. Except for the collector of the relics of John Company—Chippendale chairs, French mirrors, or Sheffield plate—there is little of art in them which cannot be better bought elsewhere, and even at her best the midday sun can find nothing in all her borders to arrest the eye and little enough to chain the imagination. The Black Hole ? Yes, it has been contingently re-discovered. The Government official has his faith fixed for him by a marble tablet and a good-intentioned reservation by Dalhousie Square. But the railed-off marble floor does not help a visitor much to re-construct the famous cellar, and, besides, the full space is partly covered by the high and ornate red walls of the new post-office. Moreover, there are so-called experts who deny its authenticity, and would place the original site of the Hole on the other side of the post-office.

There is also a tablet to Job Charnock in the garden of the old cathedral, and another to William Hamilton, who vindicated the chartered rights of the East India Company when threatened by the feeble and wastrel successors of the Great Moguls. But Madras is the real centre of this early and tentative British enterprise, and there is more human interest in the bare registers or Yale's communion plate in Fort St. George than in all that remains of our first occupation and tribulation in Calcutta. Of the splendour of bygone India there is naturally not a vestige.

But Calcutta has one unfailing charm of its own—the sunset glories of the "Hugli." It is not of her own making, except so far as her own peculiar dirtiness has contributed to the sight, but you may always find it if you will walk or drive out as the day wanes. The day-long smoke-coils from the vomiting chimneys of Howrah and Calcutta have died down, and the rich brown sediment of the sky lies in the now windless air between the city and the nobility of the western sky. The flat expanse of the maidan runs unchecked in the dusk to the very water's edge, where the ocean-going steamers lie, and from it the reflected brown-crimson splendours of the horizon and the orange and gold gradations which lead up to the faint purples and steely blues of the zenith are seen with all the unique enhancement of webbed black masts and silhouetted rigging. The tints mount and recede, Government House in the distance takes on a rich orange, and behind you Fort William stands out one moment in sepia before it falls away in the encroaching tide of evening lavender. The lights of the long string of carriages come out, and the scene is over. Short as it is, the sunset remains the most beautiful thing in the metropolis of India. Nowhere else in the world do river scenery and the fog of a manufacturing town close in such a vista of long grey-green swathes of grass edging quite up to ocean steamers of ten thousand tons, and ringed about with the great suggestions of a city.

From nowhere does one see the city itself; it lies in the background, stalking the visitor now and then from behind the vista of a street or the smoke of many chimneys, but never asserting itself as a tangible thing. Once I went round Calcutta by night. The Thagi and Dacoity Department lent me a man and gave me three hours of unguessable experiences. But it is not an expedition that it is easy for a visitor to make, and the strange glimpses of the Arabian Nights, of scenes from Port Said dancing-rooms, or of night-gambling in the cafés of Constantinople, rich and varied as they were, were foreign, too, and of necessity hid themselves strangely and securely in this modern ugly town, where nothing counts but the chances of making oneself wealthy or the hope of leaving it for ever. Sentiment—and I could almost add religion of every kind—has been reduced here to a subordination, that is a queer contradiction of the underlying superstition of most of the races that make up the population.

Socially Calcutta provides a few pleasant weeks

SUNSET FROM THE FORT, CALCUTTA.

in the year; the work of Government routine is carried on here during the cold weather—what else is there left to say of her? Little enough. It is a notable thing that she has ousted no other one of the natural capitals of India. She provides, indeed, a happy hunting-ground for the rabbit-hearted sedition of some sections of the Bengalis, but with that political achievement she is fain to rest. What Calcutta says few men care to know, in spite of the vast wealth that annually pours through her as the clearing-house of the Gulf of Bengal. There is much that is worthy of Calcutta done within her—nothing that is worthy of the capital of India. The Army and Navy Stores remain as the symbol of Calcutta. It is a place where one can buy cheap European goods pleasantly and from a fair range of choice; one's hair is cut better in Calcutta than elsewhere. The Bengal Club is the best in Asia. One remembers pleasant evenings as one passes through—passes through. There, perhaps, the truth lies. Little as any part of India can be called the permanent home of any European, Calcutta is the place beyond all others of which it is true that in the counting-house, as in the streets and law courts, in the pettiest flat as in the houses of the councillors, every white man and white woman is at the same task, counting the very hours till the days of his exile be past and done, and he shall be able to shake the dirt of Calcutta from his feet and her memory from his mind for ever.

Yet he keeps grim hold of his inheritance for his sons' sake, and hereby is the strength of English work abroad. Verily Calcutta is a great city in spite of itself.

III

Darjiling.

The road cut out of the mountain side turns a corner and the last sight of human habitation vanishes. You may slip down a few yards on to a projecting ledge of rock to get out of the way of the dust that is kicked up by the bullocks as they pass. There is no beast living that shuffles up so much dust as the common bullock. It would be a curious point for Darwin to have decided. I suppose that oxen only flourished where there was a certain amount of good and probably rather short vegetation, so that it did not matter much whether as he walked the beast dragged his feet. Camels have long learned the wisdom of planting their feet and picking them up again neatly, however fast they may be travelling; and an elephant's experience in the long jungle grass may have taught him his Agag-like methods of progression. Certainly bullocks were never intended by their Creator for work in the loose dust of an Indian-made road. Draught bullocks in the East are generally shod. The great white oxen which draw the gold and silver guns of Patiala are, I believe, shod each beast with his corresponding metal; but it must be a poor alloy of gold that is hard enough to stand such work. Here on the grassy ledge we are away from the wayside dust which hangs so heavily on every leaf, and turns to a dull, universal eucalyptus grey the richest greens beside the Himalaya roads. The matted bents mask the steep ana uncertain edges of the little plateau. Here, at a height of seven thousand feet above the sea, an almost English climate modifies considerably the trees and flowers round us, but it is chiefly in the manner of introducing hardier specimens than in entirely cutting out the tropical vegetation which has rustled past the carriages of the little toy railway that climbs up from Siliguri. Over there is a reddening patch of barberry beneath a camelia, just such a clump as adds a note of colour to a path at Belvoir; over it, incongruous but flourishing, is a tree-fern with its witch-mantle of last year's brown dead foliage.

A little farther there is a canary tree growing by the side of the path, and streamers of white orchid fall from it. It is too common here to attract much notice, and long grey lichens, like seaweed, drip from the upper branches. Yaktail grasses throw up fountains of white feathery bents in between the dark reddish and amber-coloured rocks. A couple of Tibetans pass slowly up; one, I suppose, is a woman, as her hair is done in two pigtails instead of one, and a flash of fleur-de-lys turquoise marks her ear, but it is difficult to see clearly, and there is nothing else in the dress to distinguish one from the other. Their cheeks are swollen with lumps of cheese, and their cloth-topped boots of half-raw hide are white with dust. The man is carrying a prayer-wheel, and as he walks he keeps time with the chained weight. He murmurs the eternal Tibetan formula as he goes, but the syllables are all lost in a low hum. There is a cheerful trickle of water from the split bamboo runnel beside the path, and his companion stops to drink, boldly putting her mouth to the slant cut edge of the half-pipe. It is pleasant to be so far removed from the caste prejudices of India, where, even at a wayside railway station, the boy who doles out the water must be a Brahmin, and those whom he serves must never dare touch the lip of the pitcher. There is a slight scent of incense in the air. It is, I suppose, some unseen plant of humia, but it harmonises pleasantly with the two stumpy figures muffled in thick dirty crimson cloth. They pass on their way and vanish, and the only thing which still moves in the hot air is the slant of some zig-zagging butterfly. You crush a bed of ferns as you sit down and look out over the abyss to the north.

Darjiling has many practical advantages. It is the hot-weather station for the Bengal Government, and therefore the resort also of such Calcutta society as cannot go to Simla. It is a healthy sanatorium for troops, and, besides, has a certain strategic and commercial importance because the roads that run through Sikkim to Tibet converge at the Tista bridge. As the road that runs beside the Tista falls into the river for six months in each year the Lepchas and Paharias find it, as a rule, safer to make their way up again through Pashok and the tea gardens to Darjiling, instead of tramping on beside the cold snow-curdled stream and through the 'sal' forest to Siliguri. They have little eye for natural scenery. But the one claim that Darjiling boasts which will remain in the mind of those who visit her, is that from this mountain side on which you are now sitting there is to be seen beyond all cavil or rivalry, the finest view that exists on this earth. It is generally a waste of time, and always a thankless task, to attempt to describe a view. Nothing, unless indeed one has the pen of a Ruskin, can bring home to the reader more than a mere ghost of the charm of any landscape. Yet if but one or two may thus be induced to take the risk—and a risk it is—and make the journey from Calcutta, it will have been worth while to say a few words. There is always the chance and often the certainty of cloudy weather, and many of Darjiling's visitors go back home without having seen this crowning glory of India. But such an evening as this would make amends for many days wasted here by even the busiest of globe-trotters.

Far beneath one, the mountain-side falls almost perpendicularly, though, were you to drop from the little plateau, you would be caught at once in the rich vegetation that springs wherever a seed can obtain roothold on a ledge or in a cleft. Three thousand feet below, the valley stretches out ten miles wide from the foot of the precipice. At this distance it is difficult to see much of the detail of the landscape, though one realises that, after all, there has not been entirely lost the last sign of the presence of man. Lost in the tangle of a little wood there is the flash of a white wall, which, I believe, indicates an isolated mission station. As the crow flies it must be four or five miles away—half lost in the unkempt patches of jungle which still dispute possession with the tea-fields. At this distance the tea plantations show only as regular patches of even green, more like stretches of turf than what they really are. Beyond them, the valley seems to end against a mountain side which is probably like that on which you sit, though even in this clear air every detail is at this great distance hazed about with blue. In itself this view would make the reputation of many a mountain eyrie in Europe, but it is the way in which the walls of the Himalayas close the panorama with a thousand deeply-cut ravines that lends contrast and gives it a particular beauty in the distance. Above the projection of lower cliffs, which seems to stop with curious suddenness, comes a great mass of treeless rock, indigo and ash blue, in the fading light. As the eye travels upwards to a point far higher than that on which you sit, the first outposts of the glacier ice-field are dimly seen thrusting themselves in between the pinnacles and curtains of rock. Still the eye mounts, and at last the waste of Himalayan ice crowns the scene.

Even to this distance, twenty miles away, the frozen and untrodden wilderness throws its influence. The awful cold and silence of that blue-shadowed desert of cavernous white ice chills you as you watch. Rarely indeed does some projecting point of grey rock break up through it, though here and there at its edges it washes in cold hummocks up against the stark granite walls of the mountain range, so steep that neither snow nor ice can rest upon them. There is a lavender haze over it in which details of ice-field and dark rock alike are at last lost. It is a view that cannot be paralleled on earth, and the satisfied eye ranges downwards again, perhaps traversing with the quickness of thought the aching distances that stretch between the little mission building and the grey distance of the crowning sky. You may well be satisfied with this, and if the day be a little overcast you will go away from Darjiling, feeling that in this contrast of the tropics and of the eternal ice, you have seen something that you will never forget.

But this evening, the light mists that over the valley hung balanced in the void have risen, and you will see something more, and as you look you will hardly believe that you have really seen it.

Up above the grey lavender sky that crowns the glacier-field, up in mid-heaven, up where, by rights there should be nothing but the night riding stars and constellations, separate, detached, unconnected with anything on earth, there rise in mid-heaven the rose-pink ice peaks of Kinchinjunga. Fifty miles away, yet clearer than the glacier-field below them, the crannies and clefts, the chairs and pinnacles of Kinchinjunga stand out in pale crimson glory across the lavender sky, more like some heavenly vision of an old painter than anything that can possibly be real in this world. Motionless, silent, ethereal, these untrodden peaks of mystery defy for ever the trespassing foot of man's curiosity. They hold the colour just as a great ocean shell of the South Seas glows daintily with twenty shades of pink. For us the sun is now set, but for ten minutes you may still watch from the thickening ash grey shadows of your mountain coign the set scene, immovably fixed for all the interplay of fading rose. Then Kinchinjunga dies out again, and only the dark starless patch in the patined sky will tell you all night that what you have seen is no mere vision or delusion.

Puri.

If there is one thing more than another which recalls the earliest conception which childhood ever acquired of the mysteries of India, I suppose it is the word Jaganath. I remember a volume of Tenniel's cartoons, in one of which there was a gruesome picture of the famous car being dragged along by a thousand men, while from under its tyres there lengthened a ghastly avenue of crushed and mutilated figures. In those days, before the relentless Hunter came, we used to spell it Juggernaut, but the pronunciation is the same, and the thing is the same. Why the car of Jaganath should in particular have been credited with man-slaying qualities I do not know; certain it is that there is a fine car in the temple at Puri which is regularly used, and no doubt there must always be a number of willing martyrs within the ranks of every religion, but I am inclined to think that the sheer difficulty of maintaining a foothold while five hundred men are struggling round one to help in pulling forward the ungainly vehicle accounts for most, if not all, of the lives lost beneath the wheels of the car. This is prosaic, but the truth generally is. It is worth while to go to Puri and see the Temple of Jaganath. It is only a little more than a night's run from Calcutta, and it is one of the prettiest places in all India. You can go by sea if you like, but the railway now runs from Khurda Road to Puri, and the roadstead is unsafe for vessels in even the slightest gale.

As you get out at Puri you will find the same chattering crush of natives intent upon their own business—on the whole, a law-abiding mob. If you are wise you will at once seize one of the rickety little carriages and drive off through the sand of the roads to the bungalow. If you are a great person the Viceroy's private secretary will probably have invited you to make use of the official Circuit House during your stay at Puri. As a rule in India, an official residence is to be preferred to a dak bungalow, but in this case the two are side by side, and it is impossible to imagine a pleasanter little five-roomed house than the bungalow at Puri. It is built low down upon the seashore. In winter the returning monsoon must dash the spray

THE TEMPLE OF JAGANATH, PURI.

against the very walls and windows of this little house of rest.

As I sit here and write, the long soft thunder of the sea croons eternally in the ear, and on either side the white rolling sand dunes, lightly scattered with green grass and crowned by the blue line of the dimpling sea, run south and north, this till it is hidden by the Circuit House, that till it is lost in a little venturesome wood of stunted casuarinas. The cool sea-breeze is wafted into the room—a pleasant change, indeed, from the hot and dust-laden airs that swirled and scattered the dust but yesterday in Calcutta streets. One can go out and watch the incoming waves. There are three things that men can look at together without feeling the need of speech, yea, four things that lull our human desire always to be talking. The rise and splash of the fountain, the lick and play of the flame above the tinkling red core of a coal fire, the roll-over and "lick-o'-the-lips" of a flag, and the lazy nonchalance and gather-and-fall of green waves at the seaside. What is the common source of quiet sympathy in each? A lazy and recurrent motion; but why that should have the effect it does is not easily explained. Why, that is, two men should be able to sit and smoke in silence before a fire and not before an empty grate remains a mystery.

There are not many places in India where you can watch the waves swarming in upon the beach. At Bombay you may see the big western rollers smash themselves into white jewels upon the rocks that guard the end of Malabar Point, but of sand or gravel there is none. No one ever yet went to Diamond Harbour except for the purpose of getting away from it as soon as possible. Cochin is a sea backwater, where little three-inch waves splutter and fuss along the three-foot rockery that protects the Residency lawn. Quilon is all bare rock, relieved here and there by little enclosed slopes of white sand. Of all the better known places of India, at Puri and Madras alone can one sit on the shore and watch the familiar English habits of the oldest of our friends—the sea. There is something of home-sickness in the lift and the poise and the crash and the spread in the monotonous yet infinite variety of the green fresh waves of the Bay of Bengal, and the white lace which slips down the inner slope of the green wave was surely woven by sea maidens of the Dorsetshire coast. One hundred yards out the incoming combers fret themselves upon a sandy shallow, and a momentary flash of white crests the edge of a breaking shell of yellow. I daresay the sand-bank can be seen at low tide. There is a well on the beach fifty yards from the bungalow, and better water is not drawn in India. I remember a man's story of how, off Muscat, in the Persian Gulf, sailors obtain fresh water in the middle of the sea by letting down bottles to fill themselves at the bottom, where a mighty spring hurls itself up into the brine. I daresay it is true. As a rule the Eastern tales which seem most false are the truest, the likely ones are the lies. Anyway, Tavernier has something like it.

You can walk over the sands to the great temple. There is a stretch of perhaps six hundred yards of raw fat-leaved marine plants and sandy casuarina trees before you defile through a little street of flat-roofed dilapidated mud-cottages with mongrel dogs alive with mange snarling or sleeping in the sun, and reach at last the great open space in front of the temple. On either side of you the great twenty-foot wall stretches with its Ghibelline battlements, two hundred and fifty yards perhaps in length. Up against it are huddled innumerable little shops and shanties. In the centre, thrown forward twenty yards, is the famous black pillar. This is one of the most beautifully worked things in India. From a plinth of half a dozen courses, beautifully recessed and diapered with a pattern of conventional beasts and ornament, rises the thirty-foot shaft of fluted black marble, terminated by a plain capital almost Doric in its simplicity, whereon a tiny figure of the Dawn sits all unconscious of the ludicrous disproportion between itself and its majestic pedestal. Immediately behind it is the great gate of the temple itself, flanked on either side with somewhat substantial houses. You may go up to the gate if you like, but no white man, living or dead, has ever gone through it. Even Lord Curzon, who, for half a dozen reasons, had a better claim than anyone else, and who had made a journey from Calcutta specially to see the interior of the temple, was politely but firmly refused admission. Nay, more extraordinary still, the Grand Lama of Tashi-Lhunpo, the living reincarnation of the very Buddha, of Him who was, according to the later Hindu faith, no less than the ninth and latest manifestation of Vishnu himself, was this year privately warned that he would not be allowed within the gates of Vishnu's greatest shrine. This is all very mysterious. Moreover, you will hardly get a consistent account of the temple interior even from a native who has repeatedly visited it.

Of one thing there is no doubt whatever, and for this reason alone the temple of Jaganath at Puri has an interest and a significance which attach to no other spot in India. The rules of caste in India are more binding far than the laws of the Medes and the Persians. Even a globe-trotter can hardly fail to notice, in his butterfly zigzags about this country, that time and civilisation have not relaxed in the slightest degree the stern and unbending rules which separate, in life and in death, the members of one caste from those of even the next above it or the next below. His attention will probably be called to it first by his bearer's incomprehensible explanation of why he could not obtain his food at a certain place, and his demand of half a day's holiday that he may tramp a mile to buy or eat among his own people. Nay, the truth is that the spread of civilisation has rather tightened than relaxed these relentless bands, though missionaries are loath to admit it. For with civilisation snobbishness ever walks hand in hand; and, incongruous though it may seem, the chief manner in which we have affected Indian domestic relations is by fostering an increase, not a decrease, of their social distinctions. We have encouraged even the lowest in caste to hope for some token of social distinction, some precedence which fifty years ago was undreamed of. The seed thus sown has borne strange fruit far outside the administrative and military services. We have introduced snobbishness into the East. The easiest way in India for a man to claim a status one degree higher than that to which he has a right, is by observing regulations, both positive and negative, from which, as a member of the lower caste, he had been hitherto exempt. From one end of India to the other there has been of late years a noticeable willingness on the part of a lower caste to suffer the disabilities of one somewhat higher in the scale.* Enormous sums of money have been given by wealthy low-caste Madrassis for a fleeting association with a Brahmin.

Now in Puri all caste vanishes.

The significance of this can be understood only by those who know India. This absolute reversal of all that is most sacred to India gives to Puri a

* We may smile at the social ambitions of the guileless native but it after all is the same all the world over, even among the professionally unworldly classes. There are few bishops of the Church of Rome who are to-day content to display a hat with six tassels, and few archbishops who do not claim the fifteen which by right should be borne by a Cardinal alone.

meaning which will, perhaps, never be wholly understood by any European. In Southern India there is indeed something a little like it. Once a year, during a festival—a spring festival, which corresponds roughly with the Saturnalia of ancient Rome, with certain curiously indecent rites—caste is also forgotten for the night. But here in Puri we have a place where, year in and year out, this extraordinary religious socialism is not merely tolerated but an imperative custom. Nothing can be more significant than the fact that the guardian and head of this most holy Hindu temple is the Raja of Khurda, who, by hereditary and inevitable descent, is a sweeper, the lowest of the recognised castes.

The story of the founding of the Temple of Jaganath is odd. Once upon a time, in the days of Indra-mena, King of Orissa, he was told to go to the seashore at Puri, and there dig for the long lost temple of Vishnu. It was buried nine miles deep in the sand of the shore. He found it, however, and then covered it up again. This he must have done with regret as the temple was made of solid gold. Instead, he built the present temple, and when it was finished Vishnu himself in the form of a log was washed ashore according to promise.

Then Visvakarma, the Divine Fashioner, was sent for, to carve the log into the semblance of the god. This he consented to do on condition that no one watched him at work. Indra-mena, however, could not overcome the temptation and peeped in through the chink of a door. So Visvakarma re-packed his tool-bag and went away in a huff, Divine Fashioner though he was, and that is the reason why the image was never finished. If you do not believe it, you can go to the tank and ask the world-old turtle that helped Indra-mena and still expects offerings.

Once a year this extraordinary, rudely-hacked log is carried in procession to the Garden House upon the famous car, which is thirty-five feet square and runs upon sixteen wheels. Over four thousand men pull at the ropes, and smaller cars follow after with similarly crude representations of the brother and sister of Jaganath. The road along which the car passes is a wide thoroughfare, which is completely full with pilgrims upon this annual ceremony. The Garden House, to which the idols are then taken, is a building ornamented in a manner of which Exeter Hall would not approve. There are a score of other holy festivals in the year, all of which are connected with this ugly log. The most famous is perhaps

The Temple of Jaganath, Puri.

[*Facing page* 128.

that upon which the three images are ceremonially bathed within the temple. After this they are dressed in splendid robes such as are traditionally ascribed to Rama, and elephants' trunks are attached to their faces. This is probably an ascription of wisdom to Jaganath, but even the most learned pundits are at a loss to explain many of the ceremonies connected with Puri. The truth is that the more intelligent Brahmins are well aware of the inconsistencies and follies of many of their traditions, and those who know the Hindu religion best will be the first to admit that satisfactory information as to the origin of many of its ceremonies has long ceased to be forthcoming in India.

There is little doubt that the curious connection of Buddhism with the worship of Vishnu to which I have referred is responsible for some at least of the anomalies. The swastika and the conch, both intimately connected with Northern Buddhism, are prominent ornaments upon the outer walls of the temple, and it is said that the car festival is a commemoration of Buddha's birthday.

All round the central square of the town—that is, the space in the centre of which the temple is placed—there are quarters for different trades. To the left of the main entrance you may buy saris. On the northern side, to the east, are the fruit-sellers, and to the west are the makers of brass pots. Opposite the west wall of the temple is a three-storied house from which a fairly good view may be had of what lies within the forbidden exterior wall.

The central spire of the temple of Jaganath rises to a height of one hundred and ninety-two feet; an estimate which includes the great wheel-finial of Vishnu, which is obviously nothing else than Buddha's Wheel of the Law. It is said to be nearly nine hundred years old, and this may be true of the interior of the temple, but it is clear at a glance that the hand of the restorer has played havoc with the gates and surface-decorations throughout. It is not uninteresting to remember that within this great edifice there still go on ceremonies and services in honour of the deity which, it is sufficiently well known, for primitive indecency and unrestrained orgies far surpass anything else in Indian temples of which rumour tells. But nothing is ever known outside the walls of the temple. You may hear from time to time the long-drawn scream of a brass trumpet or the continual sodden thumping of a drum, but that is all. Never is there a sign outside the walls of this thrice holy shrine of anything but the usual crowding and chattering groups or counter-streams of native workers or loafers which thicken as the afternoon wears on, and news of the trivial events of the day are exchanged in the market-place. So, after you have looked at all that you may see, you will be glad enough to go back to the bungalow and sit out the sunset. For temples are plentiful and gods are many; but this little beach where the wavelets tumble will give you a touch of England that is rare indeed in India.

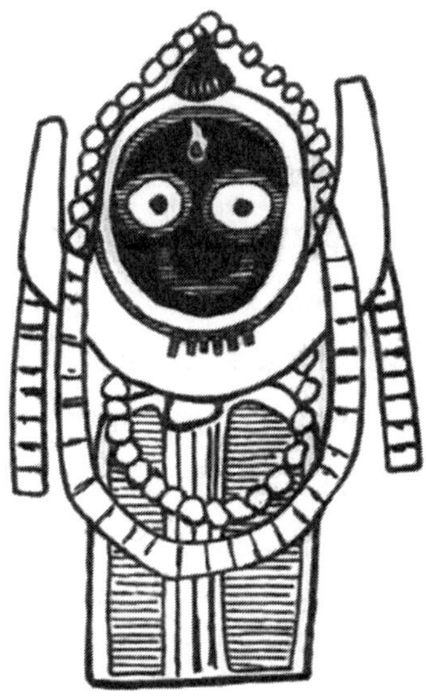

The Image of Jaganath,
by a Native Artist.

Rangoon.

BURMA sends her scouts far afield. Long before Cape Negrais comes in sight the dull, opaque green of the sea betrays, as surely as ever did the floating vegetation of the Caribbean Sea to Columbus, the near presence of one of the huge mud-saturated streams of the world. The dark, almost black, carpet that all the way from Calcutta has streamed and swirled and clouded into aquamarine beside our prow, now deepens into olive and runs through all the gamut of embrowning green till the last suggestion of fair water is lost in a flood more turbid than ever poured out seawards between the sterlings of London Bridge. So heavily charged with alluvial deposits is the water of this great sea-arm, that an ordinary bath on board ship in the Gulf of Martaban is out of the question. In this domestic way one is prepared for the long flat delta of the Irrawaddy, backed, in the far distance, by the violet combings of its southward trending

A Burmese monastery.

[*Facing page* 132.

ranges. Rangoon lies some hours upstream, and up against the turbid yellow flood the steamer ploughs for half a morning, doubling and redoubling again and again upon its course.

It is a dull landscape, and one notices the more readily, now far away to starboard, now almost at the port beam, now straight ahead, a little white flame like that of an oil lamp. Except the scrub that comes down to the river banks and a few stranded settlements of trees that here and there group themselves around a crumbling pagoda, there is no other object in all the horizon. Three hours before Rangoon is reached the tiny argent tongue teases the horizon, quivering gently in the sun and the rippling mirage; little by little the jet of light resolves itself into a flame of steady gold, and at last it rises before us clear to view, a glittering peak, five hundred feet above the river level, springing clear from the centre of the crowded busy town and smoking chimneys of Rangoon. It dominates the capital and everything around it for fifty miles; it is Rangoon itself; it is southern Buddhism; it is the most picturesque thing in all the East, and until you go you will have eyes for nothing else. It is the Shwé Dagôn.

The gulls follow us up the river as we churn

through the thickening mud; they flap behind us on wings too strong for their little cigar-like bodies; they are shaken by every stroke like an over-engined torpedo-boat. Now and then they do some trick-fishing out of sheer vanity, for no self-respecting gull could really like the mud-eating little whitebait that alone thrive in these waters. As a mere matter of curiosity, I tested the dirtiness of the stream: a pencil dipped in it vanished completely from the point of contact. It reminded me more of a wheel-fouled puddle along the line of march in the South African war than anything else. At last the Hastings shoal is reached, and the far-spread, dull towers and chimneys of Rangoon lie out before us right and left. For here are the works of the Burma Oil Company planted, and the heavy smoke-wreaths from their clustered stacks are only too well reinforced by those of the cotton factories along the river banks. It is a sharp contrast, as, except for manufacturing purposes, no chimney is ever built upon the shores of the Irrawaddy. Except in the lines of the drifting smoke the air is as sharp and clear as anywhere in Asia, and the thin, bituminous veil which fades slowly down to leeward has its own curious value in this eastern landscape; certainly it throws into higher relief the clearly-defined splendour of the Shwé Dagôn.

The temple rises upon a roughly-cornered and well-wooded platform of rock one hundred and eighty feet above the sea. Once upon a time this splendid pedestal was a surf-beaten islet far out at sea; if we may take as gospel the stories that cling about it, it must have been to an island refuge that Gautama's predecessor came. For the claim to sanctity of the Shwé Dagôn does not rest upon its connection with Prince Gautama alone. Three thousand years before—some say twenty thousand and some do not scruple to add another similar period, and yet another incarnation to its long tradition—the predecessors of the Lord Buddha left here some mortal relics upon which the first pagoda was reared. Be that as it may, in its present shape it is a vast hand-bell of gold, three hundred feet in height, planted upon a cruciform base of many degrees, forty feet above the surface of the rock.

Just where the handle joins the bell there is a strongly-cut band of lotus ornament in low relief, and above it, near the top, just where the palm would lose its grip, is a belt of silver bosses that glitter like diamonds in the sun; and at the very height is a "htee," composed in the usual way of a formal umbrella of golden rings from which, on interlacing chains, hundreds of leaf-clappered bells of jewelled gold and silver hang. Above it, set against the moving clouds, is a vane of pure gold. In this htee and vane are inset rubies which would fetch a hundred thousand pounds at Christie's. For many years all underneath this htee was gilded with gold-leaf, but as this involved a recurrent expense, of which the scaffolding demanded an even greater proportion than the gold, the trustees of the Shwé Dagôn decided, in the interests of economy, to abandon the gold-leaf and—to plate the handle of the Shwé Dagôn with sheets of solid gold! So far the upper seventy feet has been completed, at a cost which is probably known to the trustees and to the Lieutenant-Governor alone. Each sheet is about the size of a folio page, and in thickness it is about half that of a threepenny piece. Conceive what this means. Conceive the sanctity which suggested and the wealth which rendered possible this gigantic expenditure upon a matter of decorum only. But there is only one Shwé Dagôn, and what Lhasa is to the northern Buddhists among their wild and bare mountain passes, that Rangoon is to the far smaller, but also

A corner in a monastery compound.

[*Facing page* 136.

far richer, community of the southern followers of the Master.

About 1854, as the result of a persistent rumour that the centre of the Shwé Dagôn was hollowed out and was used as a treasure-house for the immense hoards of the Buddhist hierarchy, an English engineer drove a narrow shaft through the base of the pagoda. Nothing of value was found, not even an empty chamber, but as the shaft was pierced farther and farther into the interior, shell within shell of earlier Shwé Dagôns was found, till when the centre was reached no fewer than seven layers had been disclosed by the pick. The present building, which is, so to speak, the latest, and probably the last coat of this architectural onion, was finished about 1564. It stands, as has been said, on a levelled hill-top; there is a clear space all round it, such as is always needed for the processional lustrations of the Buddhist faith; but closely pressing in upon this ambulatory is a forest of smaller shrines, jostling each other like the houses of a city. Some are of Burmese mirror-mosaic, some of solid stone or plaster, roughly resembling the Shwé Dagôn itself; some are like Indian chaityas, and a few are but rude shapes of sunburnt and plastered brick. But the vast majority are made of exquisitely and intricately carved teak. None of them attain a greater height than a hundred feet, except the four great tasounds which, at the four points of the compass, rise from the plinth of the Shwé Dagôn and give pretended access to the giant.

Trees of all kinds flourish here; cocoanuts lift their feathery heads among the gilded filigree of the smaller pagodas; canary-trees, with their varicose trunks, afford refuge for scores of banked-up little shrines; and in many places, of course, the sacred fig-tree grows and flourishes exceedingly. To gain access to this platform there were originally four great stairways. One was blocked up by ourselves in the middle of the last century for strategical purposes at the time of our first occupation of Rangoon; of the others, two are of minor importance, and that facing south is now the great avenue of approach. These famous stone steps, worn to ice-like slipperiness by the traversings of many million footfalls, make a fair entrance to the holy place. Two huge whitewashed leogryphs stand guardian on the level of the road outside. Behind them a new carved roofing of teak conducts the pious pilgrim under shelter to the iron gate of the stairs themselves. From this gate the steps ascend in semi-darkness. Overhead are barbaric painted beams and carved brackets as roof succeeds to roof. On both sides, between the rough and greasy columns which support them, shops have been made and sometimes houses built in.

The arcade thus formed is one of the most interesting thoroughfares of the East. There seems almost nothing that is not sold here. Toys of a hundred sorts are there, books of gold-leaf, garlands and strings of champak flowers and marigolds, sweets, and confectionery, European picture-books and native drawings sometimes of a most devotional and repulsive type, lengths of cotton dyed in every hue known to the spectroscope, gilt caps for children, shoes, umbrellas, fruit of every kind, candles of many kinds—it is a street in itself. But the colours of the wares are eclipsed by those worn by the moving crowds. The Burmese are a sun-loving race, and the poorest wears silk. Here is a man with a black-paper umbrella that is almost an inspiration of taste—the rest of him is clad in voluminous folds of old-gold silk. He is a phoungyee, or Buddhist monk. Last year he may have been a thriving manufacturer on the Strand of Rangoon : next year he may be there again. Meanwhile, his head shaven, he adopts the beggar's life and joins at his appointed time in the muttered prayers that all day and all night ascend on incense fumes beneath the temple roofs of the Shwé Dagôn. There is a young woman, with neatly-coiled black hair, a myrtle-green jacket, and a kind of bath-towel skirt of copper silk. Here is a white-clad Hindu, there a blue and white Mohammedan, both drawn hither on as idle a bent as yourself. A child runs up and offers a trifling gift, a cowrie or a flower; she does not want your quarter-annas, but takes them with a delightful prudery. A bridal procession, with braying horns, blocks the way, and perhaps, in the foreigner's honour, the comedians of the show will give some burlesque impromptu as they pass. Chinese and Japanese frequent the platform. The former will make sure by a muttered prayer; the latter ape the European in his patronising disinterestedness. A leper crawls along to your side and asks an alms. If you give it, you will have no more peace, for these maimed and footless wretches, though in aspect they are but a bunch of disfigured and knotted limbs, will sling themselves from all quarters along the ground beside you as fast as you can walk, and you will eventually have to seek relief from their day-long persecution in flight.

The Shwé Dagôn.

[*Facing page* 140.

There is much to see round the platform. Perhaps the story of the great bell is worth re-telling. When Rangoon was first captured by us, some worthy soul thought that it was fitting that the second largest bell in the world*—it weighs over forty tons—should find a home in London. With infinite pains and the use of the most recent machinery, it was brought down from the Shwé Dagôn, put on board a special lighter, and—by an accident—dropped overboard in mid-stream. The ingenuity of the West was vainly taxed in trying to raise it from the river bed. Derricks, cranes, jacks, windlasses, donkey-engines, levers, diving suits—everything was used, and used in vain. It was impossible, and at last it was decided that no more money and trouble should be wasted on the task. Some months later a little company of yellow-robed monks came down from the Shwé Dagôn with a petition to the Governor. If they could raise the bell by their own efforts might they keep it? The Governor laughed immoderately, and promptly wrote a special permission on those lines. It made the joke of a week in Rangoon. But not for more than the week. The little Burmans came to the

* The broken and earthbound mass of metal at the Kremlin cannot compete with these real bells of Burma.

river bank and burnt incense and prayed a while. Then they set out on two great rafts and put their poor tackle of rope and bamboo-sticks together —and up came the bell, and there it is to this day under the two o'clock shadow of the great pagoda.

But, interesting as the hours of sunlight are, night is the time to see the Shwé Dagôn. There is then a charm about the huge plain, golden pinnacle, centring the darkened forest of teak and irresponsive glass mosaic, which defies analysis. Partly it may be the contrast, partly also the colour, partly the just waving crests of the cocoa-nuts, partly the faint, ever-present tinkle from the jewelled bells a hundred yards and more above our heads. Partly, perhaps, it is the quietude, that is helped, rather than hindered, by the blessed mutter of the Buddhist mass, where, round a guttering yellow candle, a small knot of monks sit intoning, their faces and their golden robes thrown into Rembrandtesque relief. Every fantastic tale that ever was told chimes in now to your exceeding liking, and even the monstrous leogryphs at every corner ache again with the breaking heart of their prototype. The gold leaf on the bô-trees' trunks gleams fitfully, and one facet from the crown of a forgotten shrine flares out a point of ruby or emerald from the peopled darkness. The scent of thick incense reeks from a newly-filled censer, where a brighter glow than usual silhouettes the seated worshippers.

Overhead the movement of the faint white gauze of cloud makes the darkened htee rock in heaven, and a far dog's bark sounds clear. There are half a dozen cheap orange and red lanterns round a swelling tree bole that has grown painfully round and enclosed a marble Buddha. The upper glint of whitened moon-lit gold vane cuts deep into sidelong Orion; even now it seems to belong rather to a mariner at sea thirty miles away, than to oneself —by day it is all his. And the last and most permanent memory one carries away from Rangoon is that of this silent and austere sentinel, surrounded by a cluster of lesser and ornate shrines, cleaving his way upward to the dark purple sky, careless of their attendance, careless of the incense and the muttered prayers, but mystically absorbed in the far-distant sea, and perhaps also in those far-distant hills on which the waves broke when the first of the legendary Buddhas halted for refuge on this lonely sea-encircled rock which is now the platform of the Shwé Dagôn.

Mandalay.

There are towns in this world whose very names are interesting. Wholly apart from their history, the mere syllables of their titles arrest attention, and one is more willing to hear idle matters concerning them than reports of interest about other less-favoured cities. It is easy, without taking thought, to suggest a round dozen of such places. One may see by the first name that it is no question of the intrinsic beauty or wealth or importance of the town, for Byzantium has an interest to which Constantinople can lay no claim. Others are Ravenna, Santa Cruz and Throndhjem, Cairo, Monterey and Samarkand, Baghdad, La Guayra and Bamborough, Aleppo perhaps, certainly Cadiz, Lhasa, and Carcassonne. Of this company is Mandalay. Long before it was wedded to a popular song the sound of Mandalay's name promised great things of Oriental mystery, barbarism, and colour. Fifty years ago stray messengers from the Court of

Chitor.

[*See page* 26.

Mandalay.

[*Facing page* 144.

Burma had already been despatched so far as to London, and their accounts of King Mindon's magnificence were supported by the tales of the rare travellers who had ventured so far inland.

There is, by the way, a tale of one of these envoys who returned to Burma from a visit to London. The King asked him whether the Europeans had any such fine architecture as Mandalay could boast. The envoy, to whom the Houses of Parliament had seemed too splendid to be real, and the Crystal Palace like the unsubstantial fabric of a dream, was sorely perplexed how to give such a truthful answer as would not offend his master. After a moment's hesitation, he replied, "Your Universal Majesty must remember that these barbarians who inhabit the uttermost parts of your Majesty's planet live in so painful and chilly a climate that I did not see even one teak tree in their land such as Burma produces in millions for the great buildings of Mandalay."

The style and title of the Kings of Burma ran in a manner which even the Shah of Persia would deem vainglorious, and it is all a part and parcel of this arrogance of place that the central spire of the palace, that which canopies the Lion Throne itself, is to this day popularly called the "Centre of the Universe" in Mandalay.* The argument is easy to follow. That which is the centre of the palace, and therefore of Mandalay—for the present bazaars near the railway station are of English construction—must needs be the centre also of Burma, of the earth, and therefore of the celestial satellites also, which plainly revolve all night round the seat of the King of the Burmese.

The throne itself is a handsome gilt projection from the inner palace wall into the throne room. It is raised several feet from the floor, and can be entered only from the back—a little extra touch of dramatic effect, that one is confident would have been adopted by Napoleon had he ever heard of it. Its name is derived from some score of small golden lions, which originally occupied the courses of the empty niches of the pedestal. The capture of the city and palace by the English troops is responsible for their absence, and, as not one of them has ever been since recovered, the probability is that the figures were—as the Burmese asserted—actually made of solid gold, which the looters preferred, for obvious reasons, to melt down as soon as possible.

The palace of Mandalay lies centrally within the four-square walls of the fort. To the east

* At the present moment it is being entirely rebuilt.

was the King's residence; to the west that of the Queen and the harem generally. Until the last year or two the apartments in which these favourites lived were used as the guest house, and I well remember staying in one of them some years ago. It was a detached house, to the only floor of which one climbed by a wide ladder, and inside it was decorated throughout with the mirror-mosaic which to this day is the most characteristic ornament of Burmese art. The dining-room of the English club had been a reception-hall, and the exquisite screens in gold and looking-glass quarrels of white and green are still there in perfect preservation. The writing-room of the club was the Lily Throne Room—the lilies also are gone—and up through the central passage, between the writing-tables and newspaper racks, and one revolving case of the "Encyclopædia Britannica," the little silk-clad Burmese used to come to press their foreheads down on the base of the throne while their thin jackets rippled under the breeze of the club punkahs overhead.

Outside, to the south, are the King's gardens. To the north are the Queen's, and these are worth a visit. In the middle is a large rectangular pool, fringed with high palms and reflecting the blaze of many-coloured flowers. It is a quiet spot, and only one object there suggests anything but tranquil and idyllic peace. This is a slightly-raised dyke, fifty yards long, which runs away from the north-east corner of the pool. It looks like a filled-in trench, and so it is. But King Thebaw lost his kingdom when, in 1879, he filled it in, for under this rough heaping of bricks and rubble and earth he had, at the suggestion of the Alenandaw Queen, Supiyalat's mother, buried alive every other soul of the Royal dynasty who could have made trouble during his reign. It is a hideous story, and was not made the pleasanter by the assurance that some of the wretches lived—visibly lived, by the movements of the dyke—for two whole days. We immediately withdrew our representative at Mandalay, which for Thebaw was the beginning of the end. Already we were in possession of Southern Burma, and an opportunity only was needed to put an end to the continual and dangerous pourparlers which were constantly exchanged between Thebaw and the French. We could not allow Upper Burma to fall into the hands of any other European Power, and we were, as the owners of Lower Burma, more or less responsible for Thebaw's fidelity to his obligations to our own subjects. Our action produced no good result, so six and a half years later we marched into Mandalay almost without a shot, and Thebaw is to-day enjoying a change which, though of less responsibility, can hardly be called one of greater freedom on the coast of the Bombay Presidency. Such is the significance of these shaded gardens; and as one leaves them to cross the wide, open spaces of burnt-up grass which have taken the place of the old, dangerous, and unhealthy native city, one is little disposed to quarrel with an annexation which has placed under our government a little people which has ever since congratulated itself upon this transference of its allegiance.

Outside the fort there is much to see. The exquisite delicacy of the Queen's Golden Monastery, the squat magnificence of Chow-tor-yar-jee-paya —this, by the way, is the way it is pronounced, not the way it is spelled; the thousand pagodas— there are only five hundred and twenty-five as a matter of accuracy; the Mingun mass of split brickwork—the biggest in the world after the Abhayagiriya pile in Ceylon—and the adjacent bell, which is the largest bell and gives the deepest note of any in the world—there is much to see, if you are anxious to see it all.

The Queen's Golden Monastery—I say it with reluctance, because superlatives are too often used by travellers—is, so far as I know, the most picturesque place in the East, probably in the world. There is one particular square yard of ground in its courtyard from which there can be obtained at the four cardinal points four distinct pictures, each in its own way unique. One is that of the annexed plate. The effect of the well-head, a weathered spire of carved brown wood, in the middle of the rich green of the palm trees, is very fine, and the more distant monastery spire of tarnished gold, worn red lacquer, and sepia-shaded timber, composes itself into one indescribable tint in bold relief against the blue. Nor is the Arakan pagoda less worth the half-hour's drive back along the railway line. Next to the Shwé Dagôn this is the most sacred temple in Burma. For good reason too: it contains the image of which the Master in person welded together the fragments into one seamless monolith, when Visvakarma himself failed to unite them. It is a large brazen idol, bigger, but, like the golden idol in Lhasa by the same sculptor, claiming to date from the lifetime of Prince Gautama. Here he sits in his recess, somewhat unkindly in feature and ungainly in

THE QUEEN'S GOLDEN MONASTERY, MANDALAY

bulk, but undeniably impressive. Before him burn the guttering candles of worship in hundreds, and a massive iron screen is drawn across the opening every night at six o'clock, waking the echoes of the colonnaded temple with the hoarse travelling of its rusty guides. But still the squatting worshippers sit on in the aisle until the candles burn low upon the rail and darkness again hides from their sight the unrelenting features. All round the central shrine is the hubbub and crowding of an ordinary Burmese bazaar. Every alley is filled with chafferers, and you may secure better mechanical wooden toys for eightpence here than half-a-crown would buy you in London. Beyond, at the back, is the holy tank, from which the best view is to be had of the gilded terraces and pinnacles of the dazzling central spire. The Arakan pagoda owes its prosperous state to-day solely to the fact that to repair it is a virtuous act and one that releases from the consequences of sin. It is one of the three great temples of Rangoon, Arakan, and Pegu respectively to which this unusual privilege attaches. The Burmese judge it but a waste of money and good intentions to put any other shrine in order, and therefore the land is dotted with the ruined simulacra of the pious erections of other generations, crumbling and lopsided, while beside them, spick and span with whitewash and somewhat garish in the sun, rise the offerings and memorials of the present day.

Yet, whatever attractions there may be waiting for you outside Mandalay you will go back to the fort and sit contentedly beside the palace walls watching the sharp, clear pinnacle of the Centre of the Universe against the amethyst of the northern sky, and listening to the silence, which the distant sound of a trotting ox-wagon, a mere speck on the road, seems only to make more oppressive. Not a leaf of the breadfruit palms or of the clambering mallows at their feet is stirred. It seems impossible that this scene of utter quiet can have been the scene of such foul barbarities and bloodthirsty superstitions. A grey squirrel jerks out from under a forgotten cactus clump and flounces back, more out of habit than real fright, the domino wings of a hoopoe flutter, a streak of luminous blue betrays a kingfisher who, for five minutes, had been motionless on a stump, watching with eagerness the tiny circles in the water below. Yet the fact remains that the foundations of the great central gates in the middle of the more than mile-long fort walls are laid upon human skeletons. The foul atrocities of Thebaw are still faintly echoed in the fireside stories of the old men. Perhaps it was only another of those cases wherein, to misquote in all reverence a well-known proverb, our opportunity came with the utter extremity of another race. To-day the Burmese are happy; happier, perhaps, as a whole, than any other race in the world, and it would do many a pessimist good to see Monsieur, Madame et Bébé—the latter a collective term out here—start for their sunset jaunt in search of fresh air and gossip along the wide streets of Mandalay. After all, it is difficult to be sad when one is wearing white silk and a tight pink turban, and one's wife and children are dazzling in lemon yellow, Venetian red, and olive green. Besides, there is always the family ring with the big, bad cabochon ruby from Mogok, which will tide over a month or two of hard times in a country which, as King Bodawpaya once neatly said, was so much the favourite of heaven that the very waters of the river added to it many square miles of new territory every year.

Madras.

The rest of India professes to be vastly diverted with Madras. There is no civilian so newly landed that he cannot poke his uncertain piece of fun at the "benighted presidency," no subaltern who does not smile at the mention of Madrassi troops. All this is wholesome enough. The plain truth is that Madras has reached a pitch of security, prosperity, and efficient administration that leaves little still to be done—little, that is, while the rest of this teeming peninsula demands attention so much more urgently in elementary departments of government. Education has been carried as far in Madras as it safely can be carried, and the bewildered English tourist's heart goes out to the street boys in her capital who speak and delight in speaking English. Irrigation in other parts learned its first steps from Madras, and though the splendid systems of the Punjab are now far more gigantic and support a hundred to Madras's ten, it yet remained for the southern engineers to conceive and carry out the principle of the Periyar dam. From one end of the presidency to the other order is perfectly kept—Madras's sneerers say easily kept indeed, but is that of necessity a reproach?—save when some Moplah community sets out on its undistinguished war-path, or a religious quarrel has embittered the relations of two Saivite communities. Taxation is better distributed here, and more cheerfully rendered, than elsewhere, and the actual returns are proof enough that in material prosperity Madras, the milch cow of India, is easily first among the provinces of the peninsula. Yet Anglo-India still diverts itself at the expense of the southern presidency.

It is worth while to consider this for a moment. The tendency is, as has been said, healthy enough in reality. A man's reach should exceed his grasp, or what is the light-blue riband of the Star of India or a seat on the Council for? Madras has long passed through that age of striving and heart-sickening anxiety in which from time to time the rest of our Asiatic Empire seems to labour still. And it is for that reason, and for that alone, that she has ceased to be interesting. There is much to administer, there is little left to achieve. No turbulent frontier province here challenges the pluck, or character, or tact of men ; no internecine quarrel between Mussulman and Hindu threatens the peace of a commissionership ; no famine or plague drains the life-blood of ten thousand square miles. Her stormy youth is passed, the new battlegrounds are a thousand miles from her and, far removed from frontier strife, Madras rests and works in peace. But she has had her *jeunesse orageuse*, her battlegrounds gave birth to an Empire, and we should never forget that there was one terrible moment when the frontiers of British India were but a gunshot from the walls of Cuddalore. If it were not encouraging to realise that upon initiative and advance the ambitions of young Anglo-India are still set as firmly as ever, there would be something sad in the fact that Clive's province is now regarded as an uninteresting backwater ; if it were not true that all things are with more pleasure chased than enjoyed, there would be something ridiculous in the lesser estimation in which is held the one and only district in India that, after many years, approximates to-day to that ideal of peace and prosperity which our rule professes as its aim, and in very truth strains every nerve to secure.

Life in Madras runs on placidly, far from the

uncertainty that lies at the core of all the enjoyment of Englishmen. The rest of the peninsula takes uncrediting example from her in almost every department of administration, and the ryot of the distant Ganges valley owes more contentment to the ripe experience of Madras than he will ever know or his local benefactor ever confess. But Madras is indifferent. With all the happiness of an unhistoried State, she goes her way rejoicing, but unsung, and almost wholly unvisited. The ignorance of Upper India in this matter is surprising —in the Punjab or the United Provinces hardly one official in two hundred has ever journeyed to Madras, and all the average Army officer knows of the south is confined to a year or two's unwilling acquaintance with Bangalore. Yet Madras teems with interest. Apart from her history—and it is all of a piece with this ignorance that Clive remains unhonoured to-day in India by even an obelisk—the racial and architectural peculiarities of the south are far more characteristic of the inhabitants than elsewhere. One of the most important reasons of this retention of individuality is that here the Mohammedan flood was stayed. Except on the sea coast, where the Gulf traders put into the quiet ports, there is little of Islam here, and caste reigns with a supremacy which is found nowhere else in India.

There is hardly a village community in the south, from the Puliahs and the Todas—outcasts from even the lowest and most despised of sweeper gatherings—to the lordly Nambutiri Brahmin, who walks along groaning aloud continually that all lesser men may clear away from his path, which is not full of quaint interest. Merias, thieves and descendants of men saved by us from being butchered on the "elephant" by the snake-eating Khonds; Arudras and Irulas, whose women are sufficiently married if a man allows one of them a whiff from the cheroot in his mouth, or a mouthful from his dinner, perhaps of roast monkey or boiled rat; Brahmins, who marry plantain trees; men of Tanjore, who secure good harvests by swinging men from trees by a hook fixed in the muscles of the back—there is not a superstition or a caste prejudice of India which does not still flourish in Madras, despite the spread of education and the easy and full railway inter-communications which within the last few years have been almost completed in many districts. Perhaps human sacrifice may still be carried on in some remote mountain tract, for all the protestation of the neighbouring tribes; certainly, some of the customs of the Malabar coast are as unnatural, if not as barbarous. The point of view is all.

Some years ago Lord Ampthill, the late Governor —to whom no small part of the continued and confirmed prosperity of the presidency of late years must, in common fairness, be ascribed—tried to explain the objections which the Indian Government entertained to the "hook-swinging" practice to which reference has been made. Finding that other considerations were urged in vain, his Excellency employed the *argumentum ad hominem*, "How would you like to be 'hook-swung' yourself?" The reply was instant but disconcerting, "If it were thought necessary, I should have no objection." The man who spoke was a man of position and reputation. In this flourishing great Eden there is still ample evidence of the vast gulf that divides not only the East from the West, but one part of the East from another. Still, in Madras there is the India that eighteenth-century travellers described—unchanged, unchangeable perhaps, certainly all the healthier for being allowed free and fair play, whatever the crooked bent of custom, myth, and tradition. Men have walked over red-hot iron bars within a drive of Government House; to secure their husbands' escape the women of the thieving Koragas still tear themselves till they faint for loss of blood; the men of the Kuravas still practise the "couvade." Yet the orderliness of the land is no whit the worse for these follies, and the inhabitants are much the happier. Indeed, it would be difficult to point to any part of all our wide dominions where our rule has proved more beneficial, and one is at a loss whether to admire or to smile at the imitative dexterity of Roman missionaries on the south-west coast, who still permit their converts to observe with all strictness the prejudices of their caste!

For the ethnologist and the student of human nature alike there is no field like that of the tribes of Southern India, and it is the last and best testimony to our wisdom that their peculiarities may be observed side by side with the prosperity and content which are too often regarded as achievable only at the cost of a partial Europeanisation of those committed to our care. Dull Madras may be, but there is no such prosperity in any State as in that which has at last curtailed the chances of personal distinction, except along the unexciting lines of a more and more perfect administration, and

MAHABALIPURAM.

to this happiness the presidency can at least lay claim.

Madras itself lies flatling along the eastern straight-edge of sand and gravel which defies the Indian Ocean. To make a harbour—the mention of Madras harbour will bring either a smile or a sneer to the lips of most marine engineers—great breakwaters have been thrown out at enormous cost into the sea. In fine weather it is safe for ships to anchor within them and disembark their cargoes and their crews, but an easterly storm-cone will send them packing out through the narrow entrance to an offing miles out at sea. Moreover, the southern breakwater serves as a groyne for the arrest of the northward-travelling coast, and the work of years may be ruined when the ramp of sand extends out to the end of the southern wall and begins to pour its deposits across the mouth of the harbour. Already it is half-way out.

Inland Madras is a fair city of green and pleasant distances. The old flavour of the Honourable Company reigns here to this day. A man will have his acres of garden or coarse lawn around his house, and the damp steamy swamps south of the city towards the Adyar are as Job Charnock left them —perhaps as they were when Saint Thomas laid down his life many centuries ago just where the stucco cathedral lifts a white spire among the palm-groves of the foreshore. Whether the legend be true or not, may be left to divines and antiquarians to decide, but its persistence here—unquestioned till the middle of the eighteenth century—adds a pleasant finish to the rare records of connection between East and West.

From Madras the most interesting excursion to be made lies thirty-five miles due south. It may be made in many ways, but the most comfortable of all is to drop down the Buckingham Canal all night in a house-boat, and find the "Seven Pagodas" half a mile away across the sandspit in the morning. There is nothing so tantalising in India as these remains on the narrow low peninsula of Mahabalipuram. Of their history little is certainly known. Every period of Indian art and religion except—and even this is not certain—the Asokan influence seems to have combined to add its relic to the curious medley, and the fact that in great measure the temples are monolithic has effectually prevented the work of one generation from being pulled down or adapted by another. Five "raths" and a stone elephant are the first objects that meet the eye. Among them is a singularly fine model—it is scarcely more—of a Buddhist vimana or storeyed monastery. The others are relics of Hindu worship, which have been, consciously or unconsciously, influenced by their Buddhist neighbour.

But it is not from these monoliths that the "Seven Pagodas" takes its name. Across the ridge of the little peninsula, all sand and casuarina, you may pick your way to where the sea breaks idly in the sun against the coast. Almost in the sea itself there still remain two of the Seven Pagodas; the others, like the drowned churches off Suffolk, are five fathoms deep half a mile out at sea. Of the two that remain, that dedicated to Siva is of great beauty and even greater archæological importance. Fergusson, whose knowledge of Indian architecture has supplied even his opponents with most of what is known on the subject, ranks this small sea-beaten vimana as only second in importance to Tanjore's huge temple. It is something to remember, one's first acquaintance with this romantically placed shrine. The sketch which is here reproduced—a certain green of almost phosphorescent intensity between emerald and olivine which the sunlit sea here wears is beyond the possibilities of colour reproduction—was made from the dark inner chamber of the temple. In this room nothing at first can be distinguished, so dazzled is the retina still with the white hot glare of the sand outside. But at last the low-relief figures on the opposite wall can be distinguished, and the huge black stump of a lingam in the centre of the small room. The contrast between these age- and smoke-darkened walls and the dancing white. and green of the unrolling surf seen below through the open doorway is one of the eerie things of India. It so far resembles sitting in a darkened opera-house and watching a scene from the "Ring," that for the first time one realises the one thing impossible on the stage—the on-sweep and mount and spray-silvered fall and spread of homing sea-waves. Their sound echoes like an insistent ground-tenor all round the chamber, and the fall of a greater or less wave is unnoticed here among the droning harmonies. Inshore, the sea is so soon sanded that it becomes olivine; beyond, its vivid green glitter serves to emphasize the dark horizon belt of cerulean from which it is separated by the white horses that break a mile away over the pinnacles and spires of the lost shrines. Thirty yards away, in the very thickest of the foam, is a green weeded rock, on which the flag pillar, so com-

HAMPI.

mon in the temples of southern India, still stands. It is now but eighteen feet in height, and in its broken solitude it adds exactly the right note of desolation to the scene.

I cannot understand why the "Seven Pagodas" has not long been exploited by some tourist agency. There is nothing else like it in the world, and, alas! it is only too easily reached from Madras. But before that evil day of notoriety comes, go and see it now—now, while still it remains as untainted by Western influence as the falls of the Brahmaputra.

"Arjuna's Penance," a series of figures of animals and men and gods cut upon a flattened rock, is of considerable extent and of some interest, and other temples and sculptures await you all over the little peninsula, but in picturesque beauty none can compare with either the Raths or the Seven Pagodas. Spend your day among them, and you will be towed back in the lingering sunset well contented with these new things in the scrap-book of your experience. If you sketch, so much the better, however badly you may do it, for the temples are worth detailed study, and you can store your memory twice as well when a pencil-stroke crystallizes and shapes an impression. But it will be waste of time to finish your sketches on the house-boat roof. It is better to lie back and watch the orange and opal die out in the west, and mark the on-coming of the vedettes and scouts of the wary battalions of heaven. Soon you will be aware of something unusual in these cold argent constellations steadily powdering the purple spaces of the sky : a moment later you will discover that in these tropics the stars in the zenith do not twinkle. There is a good reason for this, but at first it comes as a novelty which every traveller finds out for himself to his own vast self-congratulation and pleasure.

SIVA'S TEMPLE AT THE SEVEN PAGODAS.

realises that everywhere underfoot are the finest old blue Dutch tiles that ever made a collector break the last of this community's own commandments.

Half a mile away along the street is the synagogue of the Black Jews, a poorer house, but as scrupulously furnished in due ritual. These Jews represent the left-handed offspring of mixed unions, which the children of purely Jewish marriages ostracised from the chief tabernacle. In the course of centuries the Semitic traits of this body have become greatly weakened. The type is here scarcely recognisable, and the congregation of the Kadvoobagam might be of the normal Cochinese natives were it not for a certain clearness in the white of the eye, a touch of brown in the hair, and a much lower nasal index, to use the language of ethnologists. Elephantiasis is extremely common among them as well as their white brethren.

Out by the edge of the lagoon, past the Maharaja's old palace, picturesquely placed beside the White Jews' clock tower, and exquisitely frescoed in tones of ochre and Indian red, with subjects that occidentals prefer to leave unrepresented, the street of Cochin runs on between long bazaars, where the steady clang of the brazier's hammer, or the strong, sweet scent of ginger or turmeric betrays the trade of the quarter. All is dirty and careless as ever in India. Goats, with the nap worn off their knees and bloodhound ears, attitudinise upon the house steps, and the grey crows hop and jostle each other for their street quarries. A bridge over an inlet carries us down to the open grass of the point where the spidery cantilevers of the fishing machines dive and rise again in orderly gravity from before dawn till long past sunset.

The strangest features of this land are its waterways. Hidden from the unrest of the Indian Ocean by a long, linked barrier of island and reef and bar, the lazy chain of canals and lakes stretches itself for two hundred miles, and a man can go upon a surface like a mill-pool from Cochin to Trivandrum and farther still. Now salt, now brackish, and now fresh, the waterways thread their path parallel between the mountains and the sea, sometimes a shade beneath avenues of palms, sometimes spreading out into wide, shallow lakes, through which even the eighteen-inch draught of the row-barges has to be guided by forlorn stakes, jutting nakedly above the scarcely ruffled water, each a perch for cormorants. All day and all night the fourteen rowers in the body of the boat paddle on, washing

A woman of Travancore.

[*Facing page* 170.

out mightily with their mustard-spoon-like oars, and singing roughly but not unmusically as the banks slip by. Generally the helmsman starts the song. Two lines of harsh, angular Malayalam is answered by a roar from the chorus on the thwarts, a second recitative receives its proper response, a third, a fourth, and at last a fiftieth, is equally robustly capped. The phrase "Mi-ne-yarra-*ah*-si" is extremely common as a rower's cry, the boat plunging forward a good fathom on the "*ah*." Then there is a minute's silence, broken perhaps by a long-drawn "Wah!" This is not a contribution to the boat's melody, it is a warning that too fast a stroke is being set, and it is instantly responded to, the rowers coming forward with almost exaggerated slowness for the next half-dozen strokes and pulling them through with a vicious swish.

It is a land in which it seems always to be afternoon. No one is poor, no one is energetic. Here in the uttermost recesses of India old habits linger that have long been abandoned elsewhere. Women think it a slur upon their good name to wear anything above the waist, and worthy missionaries find themselves placed in a difficulty by an immemorial custom that associates the wearing of any upper garment with loose morals. Cochin and

Travancore live upon their fish and their cocoa-nuts. All day long and all year long the women beat out into a golden tangle the inner fibres of the green husk, while the men pilot huge barge-loads of the fruit along the narrow canals. If there is the faintest wind the mat-work sail is hoisted, and lying idly in the afternoon half-asleep one often starts to find a bold tattered squaresail hanging grandly overhead filtering the splendours of the sunset.

Kottyam lies some miles up a reach, away even from the main back-water. Perhaps there are few places of any interest in India so utterly unvisited. The interest of Kottyam lies in the curious settlement of Christians, who still maintain here their ancient ritual. Early in the sixth century a traveller reported in Rome that there were Christians in Ma-le, "where the pepper comes from," under a bishop who was consecrated in Persia. This is true enough to-day, except that Antioch has superseded Nineveh as the metropolis of these remote exiles. Who founded the colony? Saint Thomas, says the unanimous voice of Indian tradition. In the church at Kottyam you may see the picture of the Doubting Apostle, with his finger-tip stained yet with the blood that the spear of Longinus drew. But history still hesitates. Three Thomases may

The Synagogue of the White Jews, Cochin.

The Church, Kottyam.

[*Facing page* 172.

indeed claim the credit of being the protevangelist of India, and he who seems most likely to have handed down the familiar name in Malabar was a lusty bigamist and merchant first, and a pillar of Christianity afterwards.

The truth is that the expulsion of the followers of Nestorius by their false friend, Theodosius, in 431, created this among the other refuges in farther Asia for the persecuted sect. But the remoteness of Kottyam from civilisation and its immunity from the exterminating invasions of Timur have contributed to the preservation in this out-of-the-way spot of a last survivor of primitive Christian communities. Safe from external influences,* the tradition has been handed down under circumstances that would have been impossible elsewhere. It is curious to notice that the history of this tiny offshoot of Christianity has been a faithful reflex in miniature of mightier schools. If, after the first exile, there has been the same persecution from without, there has at least been the same intestinal warfare within the fold. Even now there are two, if not three, distinct bodies among these "Syrian" Christians, and the successive reformers

* *The Anglo-Saxon Chronicle* records that in 883 King Alfred sent Sighelm Bishop of Sherborne to the church founded by St. Thomas in India. He brought back gems and spices of great value.

on their miniature stage play as valiant a part as other and greater of their kidney. Besides these protagonists of Kottyam, there is a Syrian church here which is in full communion with Rome, but is permitted to retain many of its peculiar forms of discipline and ritual, and a company of schismatics formed in 1868; all, of course, claim to represent the true spirit that breathed in the Jacobite church. Between them, so far as antiquity of ritual is concerned, there is no question. The old sect of Kottyam is, out of all cavilling, that Christian community which represents the early ceremonial of the faith in its least amended form. No one can attend its services without realising this, and the fact that the officiating priests are of a dark race only serves to emphasise the fact that Christianity is essentially a Semitic and not a Caucasian religion.

A Mass in the old church here reminds one vaguely of the ritual in St. Julien-le-Pauvre in Paris, though the Maronite service has probably little real connection with this: bearded and married priests, the drawing and undrawing of the chancel curtain, and similar lesser points may be all there really is in common.

The curtain that hangs across the sanctuary arch

is pulled aside, and the native priest, in a full flowered cope of crimson and green silk almost concealing a plain alb and a conventionalised stole of dark red silk, confined by a sash at the waist, moves up to the altar, attended by two acolytes. After walking round the altar, to the discordant noise of every bell in the church and the rattling sistra in the hands of the acolytes, the service begins. Not only is it conducted in the Malayalam dialect—the invocation and consecration alone being in Syriac—but the Mass itself is dissimilar from anything in Europe both in the order and the manner of its progress. The kiss of peace is circulated early in the service, almost immediately after the reading of the two Epistles. A long sermon in the vernacular then gave one an opportunity of noticing the tenth-century cross let into the eastern end of the north side chapel, and the frankly Saivite ornamentation of the church itself. Yalis, monkeys, and lotus circles seem curious in a Christian church, and even St. Thomas's emblem, the peacock, seems more reminiscent of Kartikkeya or Sarasvati than of the sceptical disciple of Galilee. Against the western wall of the church there is a delightful scene. A European sportsman with gun and dog is having a good day with wild duck,

The mixing of the chalice takes place while the chancel arch curtain is again drawn forward, and the curious lustration of the altar is then performed once more, to the same discord of bells and sistra as before. One of the peculiar features of the service is that there is a solemn invocation of the Holy Spirit, by whom, and not by the priest, the sacred elements are directly consecrated. This in itself is enough to indicate the extraordinary age of the ceremonial type. The Christian priesthood of every branch of the faith was quick to see the great personal honour and political advantage to be gained by endowing the ministrant himself with this privilege, and the present claims of Rome are not indirectly based upon the right of the Catholic priests to act alone in this matter as the direct vicegerents of God. The elements are received in both kinds, the wafer being dipped in the chalice, and the Mass terminates with the filing past of the whole congregation, every adult and child receiving a touch from the priest's maniple. The use of the cope instead of the chasuble during the communion is curious as an example of a use which is now and has been from time immemorial observed at St. Paul's in London. This ancient custom has of course been abandoned, for the

Entrance to the Church, Kottyam.

[*Facing page* 176.

Italian use in modern Roman Catholic churches. A link with the past which the Romanists claim as their own is thus severed, and it rather adds to the regret that there are few or no other instances of the habit.

These few jottings of a remote Christian Mass may be of interest to some, for any custom there may still be left peculiar to the ritual of Antioch—the earliest, be it remembered, of all the churches—is more certainly preserved here than elsewhere. Remote from all other influences, from schisms, from progress, and from jealousy alike, the primitive rites of the Church are more exactly rendered at Kottyam than anywhere else in the Christian world; and as one turns out into the blinding sun of midday one feels that it was worth any exertion to reach to this tiny outcast church, which still gallantly upholds the more philosophic but less popular version of our common faith. As one leans over the low wall of the churchyard and surveys the sea of cocoa-nut palms beneath, one cannot but recall the persistent rumour that late in life Cardinal Newman confessed that Nestorius was right and Cyril wrong. The story of Roman Catholicism is pointed by single words. "Filioque" lost her the Eastern communion; "theotokos" lost her the whole body of Protestants; to-day "gravissimo" bids fair to lose her half of all she yet retains at home. But theological discussion is out of place among the rank, steaming forests of South India. Our dissensions have done much to make missionary effort in the country a well-meaning failure, which is only tolerated at home because of the ignorance of the societies concerned. The unfortunate but almost universal result is that, except on the Malabar coast, an experienced Englishman refuses to engage a Christian servant, for reasons which are perfectly well understood by his Hindu or Mohammedan fellows.

QUILON.

Hyderabad.

THERE is, after all, little in Hyderabad itself that is of interest other than that which clothes most capital towns in India. The fact that the Nizam is the premier native chief, and the widest landowner, is, of course, reflected on State occasions by a certain barbaric splendour. But the shortness of his princely pedigree and the fact that, as a Mohammedan, his very presence is a little anomalous in Southern India deprive him of that unquestioned deference which is the natural right of a Child of the Sun. The huge estate of Hyderabad is a religious enclave cut off by sheer distance from those stirring regions of the north-west, with which the deepest of all ties would otherwise connect it. There is perhaps no small advantage to ourselves in this fact. The remoteness of Southern India from the centres of interest to-day has deprived her of political significance, and the turbulent fascination of the Carnatic, that appealed so strongly to Macaulay, has long passed away, and with it has passed away the last vestige of anxiety as to anything that the great Mohammedan vassal of the British Empire might find it in his mind or within his power to do.

So Hyderabad flourishes and waxes fat. The streets of her capital are filled with merchandise and busy traffickings, and the mere scratching of the ground of her sixty million acres provides a decent subsistence for her people and wealth for her ruler. A trace of the older régime still exists, a mockery of its former self. Still the Nizam hunts with the cheetah; still he slips the hawk at its victim; still he shoots at the gold mohur; and still his elephants thrust themselves in an orderly rank through the crowds at the palace gates, still waiting for the employment that in these days rarely or never comes. The glory is departed, and the Nizam, the cleverest native in all India, and withal one of the most dignified, finds time hang heavy on his idle hands. He chooses his Ministers well. Now and then he descends upon them, and with a clear brain and unsparing vigilance tests their work whether it be good or bad. So the work goes on, not over well, because his Highness cares little for domestic reforms and trivial administration; not over badly, because no man knows what the Nizam may chance unexpectedly to do from day to day. The natural fertility of Hyderabad provides all that is necessary, though it is far from what might be obtained. And so the Nizam, chafing under the day of small things that interest him only as a means of asserting still the phantom of his autocracy, has to find other means of escaping from the ennui of his guaranteed prosperity.

It is said that he rarely goes to Golconda. Perhaps the sight of the great fortress—from which his predecessor's master drove out a race of real kings, men who played the great game on the world's stage—reminds him of the dead level of satisfactory mediocrity with which he must needs be contented in these piping times. Yet Golconda is worth many visits. It is another of those towns of which the mere names are full of romance. Jewels of great Emperors flash in the very consonants. What gems these old Indian jewels were! There are legends and records of many: some still remain.

We have all heard of the six-pound sapphire of Muttra and the six-pound three-ounce ruby of Somnaut. Shah-Jehan possessed one jewel which was valued by Tavernier at the rather quaint sum (in modern terms) of £879,245 18s. 1½d. He also possessed the Koh-i-nur, which then weighed 787½ carats. These two stones, however, may have been identical. Tavernier is not clear on this point. His account of the jewels of India is very interesting. He makes no comment upon the legends he repeats, but is quite business-like when dealing with stones he has actually seen. The "Hope" blue diamond was brought back to Europe by him. It then weighed one hundred and twelve carats. At the present moment it only weighs forty-four, but this is to be attributed to reckless cutting in Paris, where alleged splinters of it are, I believe, still to be bought.* Jehangir was offered a five-and-a-quarter ounce ruby by the Portuguese. They asked five lakhs of rupees, a sum that may approximately be represented to-day by two hundred and fifty thousand pounds, but Jehangir would not go beyond one lakh. Tavernier makes a reference to a certain pearl, originally belonging to the King of Persia, which he regards as the finest in existence. This is said to be the same as that which, early in the last century, found its way into the possession of the great Forbes firm in Bombay, and was by them

* Since writing this sentence, one of these minor stones has been brought very prominently before the world by the charge which Mme. de Rodellec de Porzic has just withdrawn against M. Greger, her guest at the time when the stone was temporarily lost.

offered to the late Lord Dudley for two thousand pounds. For some reason he did not accept the offer at the time, but the gem was too tempting, and eventually Lord Dudley was obliged to pay nearly ten thousand pounds for it. At the distribution of Lady Dudley's jewels a few years ago this single pearl fetched the sum of thirteen thousand seven hundred pounds. Another jewel with an Indian record is the large ruby owned by Lady Carew. It is about as big as a finger-tip and is uncut. Shah-Jehan's name is engraved upon it. The Orloff diamond, which is the principal jewel of the Russian Regalia, is in all probability the larger part of the great diamond of which the Koh-i-nur is the smaller. Some jewelled crystals in the green vaults in Dresden are also to be traced to the Mogul Emperors. A fragment of the "Peacock Throne" still exists in Teheran, and the Agra diamond, of a faint rose tinge, which caused some litigation a few years ago, had a trustworthy Mogul pedigree. Tavernier makes a curious reference to the screen within the Taj-Mahal. Fantastic as the idea may seem, Shah-Jehan originally intended that this last protection and ornament for his lost darling should be made in the form of a jewelled grape-vine climbing over a trellis of rubies and emeralds.

This was exhibited in the palace within the fort after only a few wreaths had been made, and then counter-ordered; and we may congratulate ourselves that the mad project was never carried out, not only because the present inlaid alabaster is infinitely more beautiful, but because, with such loot as that within it, it is doubtful indeed whether the Taj would have been allowed to remain intact for even one generation. It is a remarkable thing that, so far as is known, the actual coffins of Mumtaz-i-Mahal and of Shah-Jehan, both of which almost certainly contain extremely valuable jewels, have never been disturbed.

It is true that diamonds are not found at Golconda—they never were—true that the halls and walls and battlements are overgrown with weeds and utterly deserted, but the charm of Golconda Rock remains. It lies to the west of the modern city of Hyder, some seven miles perhaps by road, but a good deal less by the only measurements that are true in India, for the road is level and smooth, and there is hardly an uninteresting furlong all the way. The dusty compounds of the European residents, garish with the transparent flares of rocketing purple bougainvillea, or the raw scarlet of cannas, fall behind, and, for a little, the

Aurangzeb's Tomb, Roza.

Golconda.

[*Facing page* 184.

track crosses the unslaked prairie that will one day make Hyderabad a considerable factor in the world's grain market. Soon a corner is saved by a short cut through his Highness's fruit gardens, and then the main road, which had gone half a mile about to the south, carries us again straight on to the outer city wall of Golconda town. The gateway is heavily fenced with timbered and spiked doors, but, once escaped from under it, the road runs again, a white and dusty ribbon, to the foot of the Rock. On either side are the ruins of Golconda's pleasant places—fallen fronts which once sheltered either riches or learning, dainty favourites or bronzed merchant-venturers; empty halls, where music or high deliberation once reigned; broken purdahs, which need no restoration now by the austerest husband in all Islam. The crawling vines of the yellow gourd and the feathers of rank nettle-beds do their best to hide the desolation, but Golconda, save where some group of playing children or the whirr of a turning hand-mill betrays a poor home among the wreckage of royalty, is one with Nineveh.

At the Bala Hissar gate a knot of the Nizam's men spring to attention and demand the pass without which the Rock may not be visited. It is an idle restriction, for nothing less defensible than Golconda exists, but it is an assertion of royal rights, and of these the Nizam is rightly jealous. For though to our practical selves there may be little reason to forbid the freest inspection of such antiquated strongholds, the native in his heart associates a flash of arbitrary prohibition with the possession of power. You will find never a subject of his Highness's save a sentry or a mason on the slopes of Golconda Hill. Nothing, however, seems repaired except the lower gate. A steep track of hacked-out stairs leads up from beside the old arsenal walls to the citadel. Green with moss, and clothed with weeds, except along a worn, narrow track wherein the exposed ridges of rock at the turn of the treads show whitely above the reddish drifts of soil, the strait steps climb up. Trees spring out from crumbling battlements, and empty wells, overhung with mimosa and long lavender-tufted grasses, are barely recognisable beside the track. Every natural bastion of rock has been roughly shaped and worked into the scheme of fortification, sometimes so deftly that it is hard to distinguish the work of men's hands. It looks unfinished, and even in the heyday of its pride this mixture of Nature's and man's craft must have been untidy. Opposite the King's palace rises a huge unshaped pile of rock, where the chance visitor still daubs Ganesh in his niche with raddle, and leaves a marigold blossom or two to rot upon his clumsy lap. From the King's throne on the topmost roof of the Palace there is a view over seven or eight hundred square miles of the Nizam's territory, and the justice of the hackneyed saying that calls these plains, strewn with misshapen crags, knolls, and mounds, the fragments of an earlier world, is apparent.

To the north stood the famous Tombs of Golconda. Aurangzeb descended upon the place from Daulatabad, and extinguished the Shahi dynasty in the end of the seventeenth century. He carried back with him poor Thana, the last of his race, and allowed him the Chini Mahal, on the slopes of that amazing fortress hill, as his prison. It was a useless annexation. Aurangzeb, like Alexander, did but prepare the spoil for his generals to divide, and, after he had been laid to rest at Roza, near Ellora, the rise of the Nizams of Hyderabad and the Kings of Oude was at the cost of his wretched and weak-kneed successors upon the Peacock throne. But the old dynasty was effectually driven out, and these tombs are the sole memorial that its individual princes can claim. Every man, remembering his own impatience of his predecessor's vainglory, took care to build his own tomb in his own lifetime, and even unhappy Thana's cenotaph, unfinished, and partly in ruins, can still be seen. Thana sleeps beside the rock-cut corkscrew tunnel that still is the only entrance to Daulatabad. Aurangzeb put him to death to simplify the pacification of Golconda, and probably thought himself uncommonly generous to have allowed his prisoner to live in his summer palace, and at his expense, for thirteen years. So a Nizam, or "Settlement Officer," was appointed, and then in the old way, the viceregent Mayor of the Palace became in due time lord of the city also.

Looking down from the height one can trace easily enough the four minarets which stand where the main streets of Hyderabad meet. A little to the right is the huge, irregular block of the old palace; the Nizam lives elsewhere, but holds an annual banquet in his old quarters, whereto European visitors are not bidden. Perhaps some violent reaction from the wheels of unwelcome progress is then celebrated, but the next morning there, across at Secunderabad, are still the guardians of India's unbroken peace. Not all the twenty thousand men-at-arms upon whom the Nizam can call

—some say the number is nearer a lakh—shakes the silent and invisible grasp that lies over every village of India and three-fourths of the princes of India—Hyderabad included—owe their place, their fame, their wealth, their powers, their very succession, to that untrumpeted fact. Yet to a man of the type that holds Golconda and Daulatabad, uneventful assurance and stability can never be worth that one crowded hour of glorious life that must still tempt at times the inheritor of part of the gorgeous empire of the Moguls. His Highness knows the situation from every side, and recognises that it is all to his own advantage, but he would scarcely be worthy of the precedence he enjoys over all other chiefs of India if his other self did not sometimes yearn for a fair field among the clashing interests of Hindustan and no favour from his best friend, the British Government.

Gwalior.

Due south from Agra the railway runs to Jhansi. Soon after leaving the red sandstone reefs of Dholpur, and the curiously ravined and shrivelled banks of the Chambal, the country changes. The row-ridged fields of drifted and drifting sand give way to sparse patches of arable. The inevitable ak plant has been driven away from the little lots in which millet and Indian corn are sown and watered almost with the care that is bestowed upon a garden at home. Deep in the bed of wide nullahs every square yard of irrigable soil is utilised and agriculture is at higher pressure the farther south one goes. One feels the coming of a strong man's influence. At last, out of the bosom of the flat, dry, cultivated plain rises a gigantic flat rock, two miles in length, and in breadth varying between two hundred and one thousand yards.

To those who know Chitor the resemblance of Gwalior to the old citadel of Mewar is striking.

Except that Chitor is considerably longer, the general likeness is undeniable. In each case a huge rocky prominence rises abruptly from the flat plain to a height of about three hundred feet. On all sides the descent is precipitous, and a heavy and well-loopholed wall runs round the crest of each. Entrance is obtained by the slants of a road cut in the solid rock, and guarded by several strongly-fortified gateways. But Gwalior is more than a fort. It is true, that for five hundred years its chief importance lay in the fact that it presented the first barrier to an advance southwards from Agra ; but since 1886, when the British troops, which had held it intermittently for over one hundred years, were finally withdrawn, its real significance has been rather archæological than military. The Maharaja Scindia has, indeed, a few hundred men in the old defences on the top of the rock, but no one knows better than his Highness that the day of impregnability is over for such fortresses as Gwalior, and that in his splendidly-trained Imperial Service troops, quartered in the plain below, he has a weapon far worthier of his predecessors' fighting fame.

On the back of an elephant—Palace and Residency alike point an Anglo-Indian proverb for hospitality—one see-saws strenuously and slowly up the steep ascent to the main gate beside the Painted Palace. This is a fine structure, simply designed in the mass and decorated in detail with tiles of an exquisite glaze, some charged with an elephant, such a beast as the designer of the Bayeux tapestry might have traced, some splendid with blue and green peacocks, others diapered with conventional work in free and bold curves. Others again—and these are perhaps the most impressive of any—are of plain pure colour, set in bands or surfaces of utter blue so exactly of the colour of the deep mid sky overhead that they seem to make symmetrical gaps and rents and spaces in the solid stone of the palace wall. Inside there is indeed something to see and admire, some finely-chiselled capital brackets and latticed windows in the women's court, some dainty finials also along the parapet, but the foul sweet stench of the bat battalions who have had undisturbed possession of the inner rooms for centuries will drive away the hardiest of intruders. There is something apart from all other smells in that of a bat haunt. You may be prepared for, and even proof against, the more violent stenches of life; you may even be almost deficient in a sense of smell at all, but

SRIRANGAM.

this particular warm, intimate odour, that you will taste on the palate for ten minutes afterwards, and long to be sick therefor—this will yet drive you headlong. It is half psychological in its effect; one could swear that in the darkness there was crouching some warm-blooded creature of the octopus tribe; in fact, the origin of the vampire legend is clearly founded upon the suggestions of this fetid smell rather than upon the ascertained habits of those foul little beasts, which have long made Gwalior their chief capital in India.

On the flat top of the rock, and cut into its flanks, there are several things of interest. All the world knows of the gigantic statues, nude and unashamed, that excited Baber's modest anger, but, more accessible than these, there are collected in a little compound a hundred and one relics of a Buddhist age. Buddhist or Jain—who knows? The two are first cousins, and it is hard sometimes to disentangle the fragments that are left of the two faiths. Truth to tell, some of these quaint sculptures might have been carved in Egypt, or in Siam, or in Ireland, as readily as here in Central India. The bigger statues cut in the side of the precipice are comparatively modern—some are even dated as late as the fifteenth century. Looking over the strong breastwork of stone which surrounds the fort one sees the new town of Lashkar lying, white and new, in among the well irrigated and afforested lands below. Here is the real Gwalior of to-day. The page is turned for ever on all that make the rock splendid and sanguinary in history, and in Lashkar the advent of a new era is blazoned forth. And the most striking part of Lashkar is nothing less than the Maharaja himself.

Scindia is, beyond all question, the most capable and most ambitious native chief in our Indian Empire. With a mental dexterity and wealth of information that might be envied by many an expert "political" twice his age, he combines an industry which has no rival, unfortunately also scarcely a follower, in other States. Nothing that can interest or affect his wide territory is left unnoticed by the Maharaja of Gwalior. Nothing is too small or too petty to escape his direct attention and action. In the course of one short afternoon I remember his discussing the drainage of an unhealthy quarter of Lashkar; the course and prospects of yet another proposed light railway; the financial position of the club ; a new electric power station ; the proper collection and distribution of forage for his Imperial Service troops ; the destructions necessitated by the new market—the exact matter was the abolition of some adjacent stables lest the flies should spoil the wares of the worthy confectioners of Gwalior ; a patch of bad road some ten miles out towards Datia, for which the local overseer would have to supply the best of explanations ; an improvement in electric thermantidotes invented by his Highness which caused an even breeze rather than a draught, and the lessons of the Russo-Japanese war. Such a list, incomplete as it is, will show the versatility and insatiable activity of this man, the only prince, and almost the only man, in all India who adds to the nimble wit which is not uncommon there those rarest of all qualities in a Southern Asiatic—the powers of initiative, foresight, determination, and perseverance. He has put the past behind him. I asked an official at the palace about the famous Gwalior pearls ; it seemed only obvious to ask about them. They are beyond question the finest in the world, even Travancore's ranking second to these ropes and collars and sashes of exquisitely-matched sea-stones, each as large as a filbert, and ideally perfect

13*

in shape. The official saddened visibly. "Ah, his Highness will take no care of them; he will not wear them, and so they must go bad." Certainly, it required some stretch of imagination to clothe in the translucent breast-plates of pearl which his predecessor's picture bravely shows, the sturdy and alert figure which has just been driving about in a motor from one municipal improvement to another, confident, certain of touch, and, a notable thing in India, ever mindful of the life and limbs of the most tiresome of pariah dogs asleep in the fairway.

Yet the matter I have mentioned last is closest to his heart. At home or on his travels you will always find beside him ready to his hand the last book upon the science and theory of war. He is a soldier first and last. His own troops are models of discipline and organisation, and to the fact that they are his own, not ours, till the day for their employment comes, his never-failing interest in them is due. Some time ago he received a letter asking him to become honorary colonel of some corps of Central Indian horse. I heard him refuse bitterly. "Honorary colonel? No; what's the use of that? It won't bring me a step nearer active service. Now, if they had offered me the post of squadron commander instead——" His shoulders completed the sentence.

There is another matter. It cannot be doubted for a moment that Scindia's position in India, as acknowledged head and champion of all Hindu native States, is one that is yearly more and more to be recognised and reckoned with by us. It is no light thing that Rajput and Mahratta alike come to him for advice and leading. The significance is doubled when we remember that this involves at least one concession of no small importance, for Scindia is not of the royal Kshatriya caste, and he has won his pre-eminence by sheer ability and force of character. One could write much upon this man, who is, on the whole, the most remarkable character in India. Perhaps he errs on the side of over-attention to detail; it would be better to leave minor matters in responsible hands. Perhaps, also, his energy needs concentration on fewer interests, if results are to be permanent. But Scindia is either a great man or, if not, he is at least the greatest man both of and in India.

Cawnpore.

MOST people in India will assure you that Cawnpore is not worth going to see, unless, indeed, you are interested in the manufacture of tents and kaki. I suppose for the most part this is true. For the majority of people the gift of imagination is happily rather an uncommon one, and in this particular case, while on the one hand the unimaginative person would only be bored by memories and alike factories, for him, on the other, who can reconstruct in some measure the past, there is no more awful city in all the world than Cawnpore.

The Indian Mutiny of 1857 is beginning already to be an unsubstantial tale. It is not yet fifty years since that Sunday morning at Meerut, but for all that Anglo-India cares, or even remembers, it might be five hundred. Fifty years! Old men —and for that matter men not over middle-age— remember the terror that used to come into the eyes of natives who had seen our vengeance. It is a good thing that this is gone. It is not a good thing that foolishness in high places in England should delude natives into thinking that their punishment would be one whit the less were history to repeat itself to-morrow. Every now and then in some club in London, or where some long-retired veteran is revisiting the scenes of his life's work in India, you may catch still the echoes of that fearful time. It is more, perhaps, the way in which these old men regard 1857 than any stories they will care to tell. It is a fact soon realised by those who are anxious to gather the truth, while yet there are survivors, that those who passed through the Mutiny are those who will speak least and wish to think least about it. I do not suppose that any man of the force which avenged the massacres of Cawnpore has ever wished to revisit the scene. Elsewhere there is, at least, some record of successful heroism. Delhi and Lucknow stir the blood with memories of great deeds achieved, and heavy though our losses were, no one could fail to see that our hold on India, and, therefore, our power of doing good, is based directly and splendidly upon the fighting and the turmoil at these two places. But though there was heroism enough, God knows, at Cawnpore, there is not from end to end one single ray of success to lighten the ghastly story.

Do you know the tale? Have you ever cared or dared to reconstruct that awful scene? Go out from the factories towards the river and turn into the quiet of the great circular garden that now surrounds the well. Your horses will be reined in between the black gates of the garden, and at a walk, as though still following the funeral of those that lie there, you will pass on between branching trees and flowering shrubs, footed by red roses for England and rosemary for eternal remembrance. At last you will reach the mound which marks the spot of the well. We are a strange people. Perhaps we were right so entirely to alter the appearance of that awful courtyard. But the cheap German Gothic screen and claptrap angel who stands with crossed palm branches over the well-head might surely have been spared to those who hold the ground sacred. Another curious piece of foolishness is the rule which forbids the presence within the screen of a native veteran who wears the red and white Mutiny ribbon, which, on the breast of a native, ranks in Indian honour scarcely after the V.C. on a white man's tunic, and admits within it that miserable class whose cowardice and treachery has been exposed a hundred times, the so-called converts to missionary Christianity. But there is one entirely good thing here, and it is one of the best of a class which either by accident or by that touch of genius which days of national stress begets, was almost always great. Everyone knows the epitaphs upon the graves of Henry Lawrence and Hodson. This is as good. Of course, the well-head itself, a great circle of meaningless stone diapered and scarified with pattern exactly where simplicity would seem to have been obvious, is in the same deplorable state as the angel and the screen; but the inscription round it is almost perfect.

> "Sacred to the perpetual memory of a great company of Christian People, chiefly women and children, who near this spot were cruelly massacred by the followers of the rebel Nana Dhoondopunt of Bithoor, and cast the dying with the dead into the well below on the XVth day of July, MDCCCLVII."

It is almost inconceivable that the persons who possessed the infinitely good taste to write this plain, unembittered statement of the crime should have allowed the atrocious decoration of the spot to be carried out. As a matter of fact, there is only one statue in existence which entirely fills the requirements of the well at Cawnpore. It is Chantrey's work in the Stanhope Chapel at Chevening, in Kent, and those who have seen it will know why.

"Women and children. . . . . . Nana." There is the truth of the whole thing. There is the reason why men who knew it will not even to-day speak of the Indian Mutiny. More than all other places on earth, the well of Cawnpore has the gift of clairvoyance to bestow. If you will but be very quiet and humble, it may be given to you, too, to realise something that you have never understood before. Go and sit down in the shade of the trees forty yards away and then perhaps you will understand. I do not recommend the sentimentalist and the soft-hearted to challenge this experience. There are many people in the world like the lady in the "Heavenly Twins," who would drive a mile round rather than help the victims of an ugly accident. Yet in your turn, and in your degree, you may be able to understand our work in India a little better if you have the heart to go through this ordeal.

The sun is hot upon the trim, well-watered roads of the garden, and the English flowers dance merrily in their carefully tended beds. There is a light leaf-clashing wind in the tops of the mulberry trees, but you must fix your eyes and not let your attention wander from just one bright white prominence on the carving of the screen. Before long you will find that the screen is growing a little dim before your gaze. The details are being lost in an absorbent veil of gauze. After a while the white angel herself, clear for a moment as the screen seems to drift away in the haze of a mirage, becomes misty, and after rippling like a taut flag in a breeze for a minute, she, too, fades away and is gone, while beneath her the low green knoll itself is dissipated into the white glare of the morning sun, wherein the turf and gay flowers of the garden have vanished too. There is a sense of oppression —the sense of the nearness of houses and crowding people, and slowly in the space thus cleared there is compacted a shape—the thick squat mouth of a common well. It is round, and it rises some eighteen inches above the ground. It is, perhaps, four feet across within from lip to lip; there are three low steps on one side. Almost between it and yourself a triple-stemmed pipal hangs for a moment like a wraith and then is quietly materialised. It grows from a single root banked up high with earth. You may see where the much sitting of gossiping women has polished a projecting root. To the left, as you now see, stands the "House of the Woman." It is a low quadrangle of brick and plaster. Inside, as one vaguely knows from having been there, is an arcaded court. In the centre of it grows a single neem-tree. You can see the upper branches of it from where you sit overpassing the long, low roof. The side of the house that looks upon the courtyard towards the well is pierced by five windows. Everything is very silent.

If ever you wish to speak again of the Indian Mutiny with as light a heart as you have spoken of it in the past, you had better rouse yourself from the trance and go. Already the sense of horror and blood is thickening on all you see as once it thickened in the sight of Beatrice Cenci. A quick light laugh from an upper window behind you makes you quiver to the quick of your nails. The whine of a nautch begins again. If you will see this thing through—there is yet time to go—you will see the corners of the courtyard gradually fill with dark faces, and you will see three men make their way across it and open the door of the "House of the Woman." It may be that you know the story of the evening and the morning which made up that day of cold-blooded slaughter of women and children; it may be that you have read all that has ever been written by man about the Massacre of Cawnpore, but till you have seen this you will never wholly have understood. Of course, you know from the printed words in a book what happened; you know what you have been told of the sight within the house on that sunny morning. You know how the sword-cuts that missed their aim and spent themselves upon the wooden pillars inside were all low down near the floor. You knew that about two hundred women and children were butchered, and knew that, smothered in the red heaps, some of the English women lived still, but not that that hacked and multilated mother still defended her child just so—you never thought that that five-year-old boy, with red matted golden hair and eyes awake with terror was so like your own. Two dark figures are telling him to run fast and escape round the corner where a red sword is waiting for him, and you see the single slash that leaves the child headless and quivering on the ground. You will see the dragging out of English women from the house, happiest they whose faces have long been set hard by death. One by one they are thrown into the well, and those that are living still are not even killed before they too are thrown down. One of the last bodies is that of the young English girl who only yesterday faced Nana Sahib himself, and reproached him for this return for all the kindness he had received from Englishmen. Meanwhile the native soldiers of the rebel who had refused last night to do his foul work are shot down, pistolled at close range. I like to think that some of these men were thrown down the well and still lie there in that honourable company. The drone of the day-long nautch ordered by Nana Sahib whines still from the women's quarters.

Do you now wonder at the scene that took place two days later when the Scotch non-commissioned officer and twenty men of Neill's relieving force burst their way into the courtyard. It is a strange story, one of the few that I have ever had reluctantly told me by a survivor of the Mutiny. There was a minute's silence—dead silence. The sergeant moved up to the wall of the "Woman's House," and from it he picked off a little tangled mat of woman's hair, held together by the drying mass of her own blood. Very solemnly and reverently he divided it into portions, as though it had been the Bread of the Sacrament. Still in the awful silence he went down his little company, giving each man one portion, and as he did so he repeated gently to each: "One life for every hair before the sun sets." There is hardly a more awful scene in history.

You will miss all the meaning of Cawnpore if you do not understand what the incident meant to these dour, silent Scotsmen, who that evening stayed their just hands when and not before the tale of lives was accomplished. They knew themselves to be the instruments of a vengeance that was not the vengeance of man. With no uncertain voice the voices of the murdered women and children of Cawnpore cried to the stern, religious, upright General Neill and his men from Madras. There never was a more righteous or conscientious man in command of troops, yet all the world knows how he brought in the high-class Brahmins, who had aided and abetted the escaped devil Nana, and before their death made them, with their hands tied behind their backs, lick clean with their tongues the appointed three square inches of the bloody floor of the room, thus damning them in eternity as well as life.

So Cawnpore is dull! Believe me, there is no bastion of Delhi, no broken house at Lucknow, not even the well two miles away within the privet hedge that marks Wheeler's pitiful dykes—not one, not all of these tells the reason of the silence that is upon the lips of the men of eighteen-fifty-seven half so well as this low mound of grass.

Yes, people are forgetting many things, and many things it is good that they should forget, but it is not good that all should be forgotten. To this day there is hardly an official in India who has not the materials for another greased cartridge ready at his elbow on his writing-desk; and for all such, it is just as well if at some time in their Indian career they should make occasion to go to Cawnpore and understand the things that belong unto our great inheritance. We need not speak of them overmuch, but there is a danger that our tendency towards eternal forbearance may once again be misconstrued and breed another black soul like his who on the sixth day of December, 1857, disappeared from history in a flight of dust along the road that led to his own place—Bithur.

Amritsar.

Now it happened once upon a time that the Mohammedan conquerors grievously oppressed the Punjab. For many years, owing to the timidity or to the want of organisation of the Hindus, no resistance was offered, and the whole country groaned beneath the oppression of the infidels, until in the process of time a man, called Nanak Singh, of Lahore, determined, even at the cost of his life, to put an end to this misery.

For this purpose, he needed a small band of men, upon whose courage and strength of mind he could entirely rely, and, after taking much thought, he set to work to secure this small company in a way which was characteristically Eastern. One day he finished his meditations, and told his wife to collect into the house secretly seven goats and keep them in an inner room. When this had been done Nanak, with his face and beard smeared with ashes, brandishing an enormous sword and foaming at the mouth, ran out of his house into the market-place, crying aloud, "Who will be a Sikh? Who will be a Sikh?" Now there was no such thing as a Sikh in those days, and, not knowing what he meant, the good people of Lahore fled in terror from his path, thinking that the finger of God was on him. But at last, as he continued for the space of half an hour shouting and foaming at the mouth, and brandishing his great sword, and crying out, "Who will be a Sikh?" there came up the street to him a man, who said, "For me, I am tired of the misery and oppression of this world. I do not much care how the end may come. I will come with you. I will be a Sikh."

So Nanak Singh leapt upon him, and dragged him strongly with him into his house, and the people peeped from their house-tops and shuddered at the sight. And then they took courage and came again down into the streets. But Nanak took the man and put him in a room by himself. Then he called for a goat, which he slew, and he scattered the blood all over his face and body and over the face and body of the man. Then again he rushed forth into the market-place, far more horrible than before, with blood matting his hair and dripping from his sword, and still he cried out, "Who also will become a

Sikh?" And the people, thinking that he had killed his disciple, cried out upon him and ran again from his path. But in no long time there came up to him another man, whom the oppression of the Moguls had wearied of life, and he said thus and thus, saying also, "I, too, will become a Sikh." And Nanak seized him and dragged him into the house, and he did as before, and killed another goat, and smeared himself again with fresh blood. Thus did Nanak Singh six times, and even then, though his body and face were all clotted and clogged with gore, he found yet another man, who said, "I also am willing to become a Sikh." Then Nanak Singh returned into his house with this last disciple, and gathered together his little band of seven followers, and to each of them he gave a sword, and they took an oath that they would never rest till they had thrown off the yoke of the Mohammedans. Then, when they had done this, all eight of them rushed suddenly out of the house together, and they slew in the city until sunset, sparing neither man nor woman nor child of the accursed infidel faith. And men gathered to them from all sides and took the oath, and they also went out into the by-ways slaying Mohammedans.

Thus, as their own gurus say, was the faith

founded. After this they formed themselves into a band of fighting men joined together in a religious sect. They affirmed that God is one, that the worship of idols is abominable, and that all men are equal in the sight of God. These praiseworthy sentiments have become slightly weakened in the course of years: caste has crept in among them to some extent, and it is doubtful whether many idols in the world are as sincerely worshipped as the Granth-Sahib in the Golden Temple of Amritsar, the Holy Book of the Sikhs. They are intolerant of heretics, though they have a certain fellow-sympathy with the English as non-Mohammedans who—so far as they see them—are bred to the art of war. The tourist who is admitted within the walls of the Golden Temple of Amritsar must, however, enter by a side door. For most of us this is a small deprivation, but, considering that a similar restriction in force at Delhi in the Jama-Musjid is relaxed for the Viceroy and for members of the Imperial House, it was rightly not thought advisable that the Prince of Wales during his late tour through India should view the Golden Temple subject to this or any other condition. An ordinary visitor may go and, if he wishes for them, may even receive the prayers of this Church Militant by the

The Treasury Square, Amritsar.

[*Facing page* 212.

easy process of subscribing two or three rupees to the funds of the faith. He will then have the curious privilege of having his name and the exact amount of his gift cried aloud by the guru or priest in attendance, that all the long-dead priestly warriors of the sect may know that Jenkinson Sahib has in his generation and after his ability, done a kindness and a favour to the faith.

The ornamentations on the walls are exceedingly fine, but there is a certain lack of reality about this religious pavilion which strikes even a careless visitor. The truth is that the Sikhs are first and foremost a fighting race, and, therefore, it is left for those unfit by age for active service to carry on at its centre the religious practices of the faith. The ordinary Sikh regards the daily recitation of the Granth as a kind of worship vastly inferior to that of thrusting his blade "through the teeth of the strong blasphemer." Inured to hardship and accustomed to assume responsibility at a moment's notice, they are a splendid race. Not only do they form the backbone of the Indian Army, but it is hardly an exaggeration to say that they police Asia also. Next to the London policeman, with his outstretched arm, there is no more significant vision of the force of law upon earth than an impassive, bearded, six-foot Sikh, entirely careless of the gesticulating impatience of a crowd of Chinamen in Hong Kong or Rangoon. It would take too long to trace the fortunes of the Sikhs from their stern origin to the day when, under Ranjit Singh, they bade fair to share with us the Imperial crown of India. To-day they and the Rajputs are the loyallest of the races of the Eastern Empire, but those who know them best realise that under the decorous exterior of the best trained Sikh there still lurks the spirit of those who in 1765 captured Lahore and made their Mohammedan prisoners wash the floors of their own mosques with the blood of pigs.

There is a story told among them, and firmly believed, that is not without its special interest for the Englishman.

Once upon a time there were three gurus, who sat together and meditated upon the truths of their religion. They were holy men, and had times without number withstood the arguments of Islam. And as they thus meditated, there was brought to them a large bowl of milk, which was set down upon the flags of the court in which they sat. The time was not yet come for their midday refreshment, and the morning's visit had to be paid to the

Durbar Sahib or Golden Temple. Therefore, leaving the bowl of milk on the flags, the three gurus went away to make their obeisance in the holy pavilion. While they were gone a venomous snake crept from a hole in the wall and slipped within the bowl of milk. This was clearly a devil sent from Mecca, for his purpose was nothing less than that he should bite and kill the first guru who put his lips to the bowl.

But from another corner of the courtyard a small black frog had seen the wickedness of the snake, and she argued within herself, "What shall I do? For I am weak and powerless, and cannot drive the snake away, and yet I alone know that the first guru that shall drink of the milk will surely die." So she made up her mind, and in the sunshine hopped across the courtyard and leapt into the bowl of milk. And the snake, perceiving her intention, bit her and straightway she died. At that moment the gurus returned from their prayers. And as it was now time for their refreshment, they approached the bowl of milk, and were horrified to find the frog floating upon it. And they marvelled, for they saw that the frog was dead. And while they marvelled, one of them tipped up the bowl and spilt the milk, which they could not now drink, upon the flags of the courtyard, and at the bottom of the bowl they saw the snake, and they understood the matter.

Then they searched the holy books, and they discovered beyond all cavil or doubt that the frog which had done this noble thing had been foretold for many ages, and was destined to be reborn as the greatest woman in all the world, and that supreme power and grace and long life and godliness should all be hers. And that is why in all love and reverence every Sikh believes that in her previous reincarnation their Empress Victoria was a little black frog.

From a modern point of view, I am not sure that the medical work done in Amritsar is not as interesting as anything there. The statistics of plague prevention show that more successful work is being done here than elsewhere in India, but the hospitals of the town should be visited. I went with Davys to see Colonel Hendley at work. He was operating upon cataract, and that morning had sixteen cases —"About the usual number," he remarked. He is possibly the first cataract operator living, and no wonder. He has had experience which in all probability no other surgeon has ever had or can ever have, except at this centre. Indeed, in twelve

Sikh devotees at Amritsar.

[*Facing page* 216.

months Colonel Hendley has a larger practice than many of the most noted oculists of Europe can claim in ten years. There was one fine old havildar with three medals, whose turn had just come. He saluted and with military precision he obeyed the surgeon's instructions, and placed himself motionless on the table. Even for ourselves, an operation is always a little bit of a jump in the dark, and it is mightily to the credit of the British Raj that even in these matters our surgeons have come to be entirely trusted by the caste-ridden and foreigner-hating races of India. Colonel Hendley in a minute reported another successful operation.

But there was a touching little incident that morning. There always is in India. Let it never be forgotten that India is the saddest country in the world. Close under the tinsel edges of its luxury and show, there is always to be found, there has always been found, a depth of misery, against which administration and charity are alike powerless. Nay, our schemes to reduce the old accepted mortality from famine and pestilence do but increase the over-population, which is the first cause of all the trouble. We must be true to our trust, but it is folly to ignore some of the results of our altruism. While I was there a small girl of about eight was carried in in her father's arms. Colonel Hendley was busy and another surgeon made a rapid inspection of the child's eyes. With a word of encouragement he passed on. This was not his business. The child's features were refined and even beautiful, and I asked him casually what the matter was. "Smallpox pustules," said he, "formed over the pupils of both eyes; case, I fear, hopeless." He went on after a moment's pause: "They'll make away with that child. They'll never be able to get her a husband if she remains blind, so—she will go." I had once more found a case of the one inexpugnable prejudice of India. Against this, Western methods and commands break themselves vainly. Whatever may be told the officials, whatever the native Congress may claim in proof of advancing civilisation, the fact remains that India does not want girl babies and will not put itself to the cost of bringing them up unless there is some fair certainty of their getting married. In seven villages in the Basti district it was recently found that there were one hundred and four boys and only one girl.

I also went out to Tarn Taran, where Dr. Guilford took me over the leper settlement. We hear much about Father Damien in the South Seas, but here, beneath our eyes, unnoticed and unpraised, there is being given a personal devotion that is hardly less than his. Besides being the first authority upon the Sikh religion and history, Dr. Guilford is the resident physician of the leper settlement at Tarn Taran. This refuge dates back to the time of Arjan Singh, who compiled the Adi Granth and was himself a leper. As usual a little crop of picturesque legends springs up round the still waters of the tank here. One strangely modern in tone is that of its discovery. A poor woman, the wife of a leper, came crying bitterly to Arjan, saying that, helpless and repulsive as her husband had been, she had yet loved him and cared for him, and that he had fallen into the tank at Tarn Taran, and out of it again had come a man, young and clean and in the prime of life, who called her wife. But she had rather have once again her old unclean husband, whom she knew, and who was bound to her by a thousand ties of helplessness.

There is little or nothing horrible at this settlement; only an intense and all-absorbing pity overcomes one for those wretched men and women upon whom destiny has borne so heavily. The "leonine" symptoms are rare here, the hands and feet suffer most. One feels an even more overwhelming compassion for the children. These children of leper parents are born as clean in the blood as any in Mayfair. Until the age of eight, or thereabouts, they play about in the settlements without a taint, and could they be taken away early their cleanness would be almost certain. But in India the non-caste English may not take away children from their parents. For the best reason in the world—and is not this the best?—it would be still an intolerable outrage. So these children remain, and one day Dr. Guilford will find on the little brown back a curious pattern like a map, in a somewhat darker tint than the rest of the flesh. After that the child is doomed, and no care or skill on earth can save him. It is a miserable remembrance that one takes away from Tarn Taran. One of the last things one passes is the open-sided church, with its luffer-boards in place of glass. For this there is, alas, reason enough. Out in the open air one notices little, but once shut up in a room with lepers the offensive smell is overpowering, and even the stout heart of the Doctor quailed a little before this ventilated church was built.

The road back to Amritsar is almost straight. To the right one can see the first beginnings of the new light railroad, which will go far to open up this almost unvisited part of the Punjab. It is curious to see native navvies working two hundred yards away at their most modern of all tasks, while beside the road stands the obelisk that marks the spot where the great Guru's head was taken off by the infidel enemies. Through them, however, headless as he was, he still hacked his victorious way for four miles to the gates of Amritsar, leaving behind him a wake of dead. If you want legends of India, go to the Punjab, and as you idly drive along between the fields of cotton or maize, with the sickle-winged parrokeets cutting lines of curving green fire in front of you, you will be as ready to believe them—as willing, at any rate, to let them go unquestioned—as any child of this much-disputed soil.

Bikanir.

This is a strange place indeed. If the dry tides of the great Indian desert are now threatening the green luxuriance of Jaipur, Bikanir stands like another Rockall in the full bosom of that glaring and waterless expanse. Here there are no trees, except a few meagre bebel thorns and here and there a row of dusty nasturtiums cherished with an extravagance that is almost sinful from the scanty sources of Bikanir water. It is the wells here which bring home to one first the appalling arid desolation of this artificial town. Every traveller in India has gone through the mild fascination caused by the never-ending climb and descent of the bullocks drawing water from a well. The principle is as simple as anything can well be. The mussuk, or heavy leather bucket, is helped out of the well by gravitation. The bullocks probably find it quite as irksome to reclimb up the slant, when the mussuk is emptied and is again descending for another load, as to pull up the seventy or eighty pounds of water during their returning downward carry. This slant, of course, is in direct proportion to the depth of the surface of the water. In general, these slants are from fifteen to twenty yards long. At Bikanir the water is three hundred feet below the surface of the soil, and, of course, to pull up the water the bullocks have to go and return an equivalent journey every time the mussuk rises to the top of the well and descends again. The accompanying illustration will show the extraordinary labour that is thus performed by these patient beasts. Under these circumstances, it is with difficulty that enough water is secured for the mere purpose of quenching the thirst of the good inhabitants of Bikanir.

Their ceremonial ablutions must be seriously curtailed. The accepted description of Bikanir by the globe-trotter is an "oasis." This is a wrong use of the word. There is no visible water. There is nothing to justify, or even make possible, the presence of a town in the centre of this vast waste of gravel and sand, except the underground springs, which afford a bare subsistence for the descendants of those who in other days fled before the land-wasting of two successive conquerors.

His Highness the Maharaja of Bikanir has two titles. The first is King of the Desert—a reference to a curious old story that Bikanir only came to the help of his brother Rajputs on the famous campaign against the Mogul power in Gujerat on condition that for one day he was acclaimed by this high-sounding title. The last occasion on which it was ceremoniously accorded to him was on the date of the departure of the present Maharaja to take part with his men in the campaign for the relief of the Pekin Legation in 1900. Then the railway station of Calcutta resounded with cries of this splendid title, raised in no small part by the local banias. The second title which his Highness enjoys in popular parlance is that of the King of the Banias. At first sight, anything less congruous than the city-haunting, account-keeping, and somewhat petty-souled race of usurers and the strong, independent and open-air loving men of the great desert can hardly be imagined. But a walk through the streets of Bikanir will supply the missing link. The banias along the west of India, like the Jews in Europe and the Armenians in Asia-Minor, commercially akin, have in their turn experienced the same fate of persistent persecution. So bitter was this at one time, that the banias of the wealthier class

City Gate, Bikanir.

[*Facing page 224.*

migrated to this inaccessible spot, and the abundance of beautifully-built red stone houses in this arid outpost of human life is one of the most remarkable things about Bikanir.

The walls of the town are still in good preservation, and one of the gates remains to this day untouched over two hundred years. It is a tempting subject for a sketch. The cusped and battlemented portal, of a red ochre, is flanked by a substantial guard-house on either side, and under the arch, framed by the shadowed ceiling of the vaulted tunnel, there is as pretty a glimpse as could be wished of the long pale stretch of desert, studded here and there with clean-cut block-houses, square and white, and arched over with the white glare of the sky just tinged with blue where the line of the keystone cuts it. Under it, quivering in the mirage that thrums like a violin string over the surface of the desert from dawn to sunset, stretches the waste to the purple of the horizon.

The railway now runs up to Bikanir. You can to-day take train from Merta Road, somewhere between Jaipur and Jodhpur. But within this year they have had to dig out the railway lines three times already from the drifts of sand that are always accumulating in even the shallowest of cuttings, and a railway engineer of Bikanir told me that the expense would probably prove too great. It is curious that, though these steel rails may have to be abandoned, though Bikanir, which has enjoyed this momentary contact with the civilised world, may again be shut off from all human communication, except that of camels and carts, such as it knew in the days of Shahjehan, yet the railway, for all its neglect, will remain ready for disinterment by any large-souled Maharaja in time to come. For nothing rusts in Bikanir. There is not one speck of rust upon any one sword blade or ring of chain armour in all the armouries of the city. The mail that was worn last year when the Prince of Wales visited Bikanir was two hundred years old, and had, indeed, needed nothing save a repair to a broken link from that day to this. In the Maharaja's own collection there are some fine Andrea Ferrara blades, and it is safe to assert that not one specimen of the great smith's work exists in Europe to-day in anything like the untarnished and perfect condition of those in this remote collection.

There is a strange prejudice here which is so often found at Rajputana. The Maharaja, by tradition and by preference, has built himself a new palace.

Gossips in Bikanir.

Drawing water : Bikanir.

[*Facing page* 226.

In old days, a new chief contented himself with adding a few rooms for his own personal use to the great palace of his ancestors in the town. The present ruler has elected to build himself an entirely new residence, a mile outside the walls. This, in a way, affords a more striking contrast than anything else in Bikanir. If Jaipur is the town that Solomon transplanted, this house is nothing less than the palace which Aladdin's wicked uncle deported into the desert by a rub of the lamp—the same palace which Aladdin had at a similar insignificant outlay of trouble built for his bride in a single night. This, believe me, is the very palace. The story that Aladdin moved it back again must be untrue. They say here that it was built from the designs of Sir Swinton Jacob, but everyone will agree with my version who has once seen the rose-coloured walls, terraces, cupolas, and infinitely fine fretted windows of this palace, rising, without an interposition of even so much grass or herbage as a Brixton villa can boast of, straight out of the gaunt emptiness and still moving sand of the Great Indian Desert.

It would be hard to find a greater contrast or incongruity than that one experiences in leaving the rooms of this palace luxuriously furnished with every European invention, equipped with the latest comforts of the West, served by telephones innumerable and lighted throughout by electricity —and then finding one's self obliged to allow full room for the passage of a carriage drawn by two elephants along the high road leading to the town, escorted by men in full chain armour upon camels as well drilled as any cavalry horse in Europe. Camels are, indeed, the best-known production of Bikanir. They are the finest of the Indian breed, and the Maharaja has, by careful selection, produced a class which, in its way, is as remarkable as that of the horses of Jodhpur. You will never do much with your camel in the way of beauty. There is an old story that when God, in the Garden of Eden, had finished making the animals, and had sent them up to Adam to be named, our first father, moved by a generous spirit of emulation, asked whether he might be allowed to make an animal too. I do not know what opinion the reader may have upon the strange question raised by Sir Oliver Lodge as to whether the conception of a deity excludes any such attribute as a sense of humour. But I like to think of a quiet smile upon Jehovah's face as he gave Adam permission to attempt the job. For some days Adam wrestled with the problem, and finally led up for the approval of his Creator the first of the breed of camels. I like to feel that there was laughter in the courts of Heaven that morning. But repulsively ugly as a camel is, with eyes and eyelashes that remind one of the Jabbawock, with supercilious and flapping lips, with methods of fighting and expostulation that are impossibly ungraceful, and with housemaid's knee in patches all over his body, there is still much to be said for this ungainly beast.

The Maharaja's palace is a vast structure of white walls and arcaded galleries. Tourists are invited to admire certain rooms, the walls of which are ornamented with pieces of broken willow-pattern plate. The tale that one Maharaja broke up into small pieces his priceless blue china for this purpose is luckily untrue. Upon examination, most of these pieces of crockery betray an unmistakable European and even a mechanical colour-printing origin. The finest things in the palace are the armoury with the specimens of cut steel, which are perhaps without parallel in India, and the gesso ornamentation of the halls of audience and the library. The latter contains one Persian manuscript of the Leilet-wa-Mejnoon, of which the illumination is very remarkable. There is an ornamented circle at the beginning of the manuscript, which for minute and intricate detail is only surpassed by the Irish school of miniaturists of the seventh century. There is little else in the halls which repays careful inspection. The town of Bikanir is always interesting. Upon the walls of the more important houses there are painted spirited and warlike frescoes, in a manner which instantly recalls the Bayeux tapestry; and the Cloth Market Street, where one may buy saris of yellow and orange, and cadmium, and a score of other tints, is one that will attract a visitor day after day. At the jail, you may buy carpets of excellent manufacture and curious leather bottles made of camel skin much over-decorated with blue and red and gold.

But the charm of Bikanir lies rather in its unique and clear air than in anything else. It may be that in a few months it will be a difficult thing to make a journey to the desert city, but so long as the railway remains in working order it will be a pity not to make this easy expedition from more favoured spots of India. There is but one place in India that is more removed from the greenery one associates with civilisation, and that is Jaisul-

A street in Bikanir.

[*Facing page* 230.

mir, where there is little that can repay a visitor. From Bikanir the railway lines run on north to Lahore, and should one tire of the tedious journey that must be made, the curious atmosphere and even more curious life of this community of the wilderness, it is an easy thing to escape to the capital of the Punjab and enjoy again the hotels and gardens and lawns of Anglo-India.

Benares.

THEY brought her down not unkindly to the burning-ghat. Her little almost childlike body was given over duly to the headman. For over an hour he has been ready for her, and without more ceremony than a sprinkling of Ganges water and the placing of a few grains of rice inside the lips, all that is left of poor little Yaradhani is laid out upon the pile of logs that is to be her funeral pyre. Her relations had brought her down wrapped in a cloth which they were evidently loath to lose. With almost brutal rapidity the woman possessed herself of the cloth, leaving the tiny limp brown body naked on the logs. She and her companion then shuffled off and Yaradhani was left to make her last great journey alone.

After all, she had not been treated so badly. There had even been a few months of real happiness in that little nineteen-year-long life. Of course, she knew that the end might come at any time after

THE BURNING GHAT, BENARES.

her husband found that she was not going to present him with a child, but he was not unkindly, and things had gone well until the other woman came. From that moment the girl knew that her days were numbered. After all, she did not think it was unfair. A man must have a son and heir to help him across the fiery gap which divides this world from the next, and if one woman could not give him one, why it was not unreasonable that he should replace her by another. I wonder whether the Western mind has ever understood, or will ever understand, how entirely reasonable, from an Oriental point of view, Sarah's action was in giving her Egyptian handmaid to Abraham. We in Europe have gone so far beyond that primitive conception of the first duty of a woman that there are probably few Europeans who would not be scandalised at the moral standard which permitted and even lauded the substitution of Hagar for Sarah, and it is therefore useless to explain or expect understanding. If one may believe all one hears, the tendency now shown is in a quite opposite direction. But civilised persons in the West must take it for granted that such an action as Abraham's is to this day regarded as natural in every corner of India. Yaradhani, poor soul, did not grumble against fate, and lying there nestled upon the rough logs of her last bed one could almost catch a sigh of contentment, and even of pride, that her husband had kept his word, and that, though he had found no use for her on earth, he had really sent her to be burned beside the mother of all rivers in the most sacred of all holy precincts. She had exacted the promise from him in some tender mood many years ago, soon, indeed, after her mother had sent her over for the first time to the house of the fourteen-year-old husband, to whom she had even then been married seven years. Yaradhani lying there in the burning-ghat, her life's dream accomplished, little knew how strenuously her husband had tried to evade the fulfilment of his promise. It was an expensive business. You could not get even that frail little body transported two hundred miles without some cost, and if it had not been that the village Brahmin, to whom Yaradhani had once told of the promise with pride and almost with joy, had insisted, for his own profit, upon the fulfilment of the vow, it is possible that Yaradhani might after all have been cheaply burned at the nearest cemetery. As it was, to save expense, she had been taken to Benares before the end came. As to that end-coming there was not, however, to be any doubt, and the two women who accompanied the body to the burning-ghat understood their orders.

All this seems cold-hearted and horrible to a generation which has forgotten, perhaps, many brutal things in the past history of England, but one thing may be said. It is possible that the permanence of a race is in almost direct ratio to the small value it sets upon the life of the individual, and there can be little doubt that nowadays we are in danger of losing much through the exaggerated estimate which it is the modern tendency to place upon the value of the individual's life. However, this is no place to preach a sermon on the text provided by little Yaradhani as she lies contentedly on her pyre waiting the application of the sacred torch. Three yards away the sacred water of the filthy Ganges heaved within a light boom of bamboo. It was mud-stained and a heavy coat of black wood ash stagnated upon it, marked here and there with marigolds and red powder. The headman lays two or three more logs slanting across her, and then with a shrug of his shoulders tells his small seven-year-old son to light the mass of wood shavings on which the pyre has been built up. For his own part, he was due elsewhere across the ghat. A far more important personage than Yaradhani awaited his attention. It was the late Prime Minister of a great Maharaja in the plains. Even now the body of the great man was being ceremonially borne down the steps with the women muffled from head to foot in white, wailing continually, and the dead man's son ready to set with his own hand the fire to his father's body. There was much money to be gained here, and no more time could be wasted over a mere woman. So his little son, squatting on his hams, was left to poke the burning torch into the pyre. There was an instant response, and a great flame licked upwards through the logs. The pyre was well alight, and at the first touch of the kindly flame Yaradhani seemed to snuggle down almost with relief among the splinters of the wood for which she had longed.

That is Benares. They do many other things in this great and religious centre. They make atrocious brasswork; they weave the most beautiful kinkhabs in the world. Benares sword-blades are known all through the Ganges Valley, and the political agitations which sometimes demand the attention of Calcutta find in Benares also a congenial home. But Benares' real life and

The only Temple to Brahma in India : on the shores of Pushkar Lake.

[*Facing page* 236.

significance is religious alone. The worship of Siva, the subtlest, and in some ways the most advanced, of all conceptions of a deity, is centred eternally in this strange and unwholesome town. It is curious to think that to the strange little mind of Yaradhani some of the more advanced conceptions of scientific theology had been as simple as they are as yet unintelligible to the ordinary European mind. There are very few travellers in India who can claim that they understand the attributes of this member of the Trinity. He is the god of death; he is the god, also, of reproduction and of life. There is no question more frequently asked by any European visitor to India who takes what is called an intelligent interest in the religion of the country than the clue to the reasoning which has given to one and the same member of the Trinity such apparently contradictory spheres of action. Brahma is the Creator,* Vishnu is the Preserver. Why, then, should both death and reproduction be the joint and inconsistent cares of Siva? Not one in a hundred visitors to the country, unless their imagination has been quickened by reading

* In all India there is but one temple—beside Pushkar lake—to Brahma. As a curiosity I have given a photograph of it. Two reasons are given by Hindus, but the really remarkable thing is its parallel in Christianity. No church is dedicated to the first person of our Trinity either.

Chevrillon's book, or some other of the few volumes which help to make Indian life a living thing, ever takes the trouble to reconstruct to himself, so far as he may, the true attitude of a native towards his religion. Yet Yaradhani herself, as an article of her creed, had long understood the scientific truth that without struggle and death life cannot be. Siva is the foreword of all that truth which Darwin published, and the doctrine of the survival of the fittest can hardly be symbolised better than by the trident which is Siva's own particular emblem.

Yet in its Indian home what a foul religion this is. Benares itself fitly symbolises the great faith which finds itself centred there. Dark and damp and narrow are her entries and her streets foul-smelling with hot and luscious stenches. The marigold, the fit symbol of lust, flares in daisy chains along her every street, and in the hot and stagnant courts both air and sun are shut off by the dense foliage overhead of her matted pipals. You will find sleek bulls, good-natured pirates of the fruit and confectionery stalls, living emblems of virility, rambling loose in her narrowest streets, and the crash of cymbals and the monotone of drums make hideous discord from behind walls into which

The greatest Temple to Siva: the Golden Temple, Benares.

The largest Temple in India: a view of the forbidden sanctuary of Vishnu's Temple, Srirangam.

[*Facing page* 238.

the wholesome light of day has never penetrated. No centre of Indian life has been less affected by our presence than Benares. The European quarter lies two miles away near the railway station, and most visitors know little more of this labyrinth of dirty and fœtid passages and stairs and courts and tunnels, which, like a human warren, undermines the mass of buildings on the river-bank, than can be seen from the platform of a river-boat or a hasty plunge into the slums which encircle the Golden Temple. Yet if you would understand the life of India this is the place where, and where only, it can be learned.

The burning-ghats down by the river are the most important of all. Here beside the flood which washes away all sin the black mire of wood-ash stains and scums the water yards out from the shore. The place is stagnant and dirty. There is here no pretension at ornamentation, or even of dignity. The men who officiate are of a low caste, yet without their touch the holiest Brahmin cannot to the full reap the priceless privilege of Benares. There is squalor in every corner of the bank. Heaps of decaying flowers carelessly raked aside give out a pestilent odour, for which, however, one is almost thankful in that it somewhat masks the even more terrible smell that hangs always in the air. Wailing and lamentation are the only sounds that mingle with the crackle of the flames or the occasional report and fierce hiss of some expiring log of wood. There are perhaps four or five idle sightseers squatting along a projecting parapet, but their interest is of the most casual description. You will find it at first a hard thing to understand the real and awful sanctity of this littered and neglected spot. Yet here is the centre of Hinduism. The ground is as holy as the water which laps up against it, and the fortunate man or woman whose body is burnt with due ceremony here knows—as surely as the Mussulman knows it who dies in battle against the heretic, as surely as the Buddhist knows it who falls fainting upon the Ling-Khor at Lhasa, as surely as the Catholic who dies after plenary absolution by the Church knows it—that eternal happiness is reserved for him beyond all doubt and hesitation, whatever their sin or negligence on earth. Sivaism is the centre round which all Hinduism revolves, and you will learn more by seeking to understand the significance to a Hindu of this grim cremation ground than by loitering for months among the most famous temples and shrines of India.

The Lion Pillar recently found at Sarnath, near Benares.

[*Facing page* 240.

Buddh-Gaya.

SEVEN miles south of Gaya lies that one spot which, if votes could decide the matter, is out of all question the holiest of all holies, the most sacred rood of ground upon the surface of the earth. For the Buddhists of Asia this is their Gethsemane, Bethlehem and their Calvary; this is their Mecca and their Medina. For this is no other place than that wherein the most Blessed Master received enlightenment and the knowledge that at last upon him had fallen that divinity which ten thousand years before had vanished from the earth. One may tread the same road by the side of the River Phalgu as that which Prince Gautama trod fainting, disheartened and discredited. We may be sure, too, that the landscape is much the same as that which greeted his eyes also. Then, as now, the patient yokes of oxen turned at the end of their furrow in the hot earth which needs but the three-inch scratching of a primitive plough. Then, as now, the dipping poles of the wells worked in unison, scattered in couples and threes over the landscape; and then, as now, the mynas chattered and flirted white wings in the hot roadside dust. Twenty-four centuries have made less change along this country road than twenty-four months in the outskirts of one of the larger towns of India to-day. The wide level sands of the Phalgu, with hardly a trickle of water, seeking a shelter against the eastern bank, are revealed and hidden now and again as we jolt along the road to Buddh-Gaya. If you are looking you may see somewhere along the dusty road a flash of salmon-pink that will betray the presence of one of the chelas or disciples of the Hindu owner of the land on which Buddh-Gaya stands.

The last mile of the journey is particularly beautiful. The road passes over a tiny nek between two grassy folds, and a pinnacle of golden brown overtops the shisham and banyan trees. A few straggling houses appear through the trees on either side of the road a quarter of a mile ahead. Those on the left are the farthest outposts of the Mahant's own house. This worthy official, of a shrewd but not unpleasant type, is well content to combine the collection of alms from devout pilgrims of every creed with the reputation and sanctity which involves the person of the Keeper of the Shrine. The fact that the shrine of which he is the guardian has no original connection whatever with his own faith is a matter of small moment to him. It is his property, and he has done wise in hedging about his anomalous position with all the ceremony that he can. His ancestors were of the same opinion, and the present Mahant has in his possession a curious document, which oddly emphasises the strangeness of his position, for he, a Hindu, bases his claim to the guardianship of a Buddhist shrine, now under the control of a Christian Government, upon a grant made to his ancestor by a Mohammedan emperor.

One turns sharply up a little hill to the right, and at the top one looks down into a wooded amphitheatre enclosed on every side by a low wall with a gate in the middle. In the centre of this natural basin rises the temple of Buddh-Gaya. Externally it consists now of a highly-decorated plinth about twenty feet high, from which again springs the central spire, over one hundred and fifty feet in height, rising in stages like a South Indian temple, each course set about with plaques and fluted pillars in set panels and grotesques. At each of the four corners of the plinth is a pyramid-crowned cell perhaps eight feet square externally. The construction of Buddh-Gaya temple is interesting because it represents, and in Northern India is almost alone in representing, the old Indian form of the vihara or Buddhist monastery. There are two storeys, and though it is thought that Buddh-Gaya was never actually used for that purpose, in arrangement it symbolises the primitive distribution of the rooms used as dormitories for the monks, set about and over the central chamber of worship which contained the great image of Buddah, just as may be found in Tibet to this day. This construction may be well seen from the upper edge of the hollow.

We look down into the wide, tree-covered bowl, in the centre of which is the temple. It is cumbered about on all sides with an infinite number of small shrines, dagobas and stupas, set up at one date or another by the pious, but now for the most part mutilated or in fragments. The usual entrance is by the steps descending from the northern edge of the amphitheatre. To the right at the bottom is a wide concreted floor overhung by a large pipal. This is the traditional place of worship for the Hindu pilgrims to the shrine. Until the visit of

Buddh-Gaya.

Asoka's Railing, Buddh-Gaya.

[*Facing page* 244.

the Tashi Lama last December no Hindu service took place under the other sacred tree—that within the temple enclosure. This is a point which may be of importance in the future. The tree first mentioned, that which is identified with Hindu ritual, grows entirely outside the sacred limits of the Buddhist shrine, as indicated by the still remaining fragments of a great red sandstone railing.

Passing on to the temple itself, one enters it with increasing reverence and expectation, only to see the name of a certain worthy Lieutenant-Governor of Bengal conspicuously advertised in company with those of the architects who were responsible for the restoration of Buddh-Gaya thirty years ago. This desecration, for it is hardly less, is one of the things which the better taste of modern days will surely rectify. No one who knows what sound work was done by Sir Ashley Eden in all parts of his province will do other than regret that it should be his name which thus vulgarly obtrudes itself upon the gaze of the Buddhist who, after many months of travel, finds himself at last, though it may be only as a stranger and an outcast, upon the threshold of the Holiest of all Holies.

Inside the middle of the temple is a square unlighted chamber about fifteen feet by twenty. Upon an altar facing the door is raised a great image of Buddha. It is true that the Hindus have desecrated the august countenance with the tilak or sect-mark of Vishnu, but the significance of the place remains unmarred.* There in the very spot where the Buddha sits upon the altar—set up, perhaps, within the Master's lifetime to mark it beyond all possibility of doubt or argument—there, two thousand four hundred years ago, Prince Gautama, beneath the leaves of the famous pipal, wrestled his last with the lusts of the world, the temptations of the flesh and the wiles of the devil; and there he received in humility and awe the annunciation that God was now born again in this world and in his own person. The most bigoted of Christian missionaries cannot but feel a thrill in looking upon the birthplace of a religion which has set upon a better Way more souls than can be boasted by any other faith on earth, and which in no small measure paved the way in Syria for that Christian faith which owes

* That the Hindus have painted the marks of Vishnu on Buddha, and, worse still, have set up so close to the "Diamond Throne" a great stone lingam, seems an insult intolerable to be borne. It is not to the credit of our boasted religious toleration that we should have allowed this obscene insult to be inflicted by one set of our Indian subjects upon another.

as many of its highest teachings to it as to its other great forerunner, the Mosaic Law.

Here, beyond all dispute, here exactly and here eternally, so long as the world lasts, is known and marked the exact spot where this great faith began. When Prince Gautama knew his divinity he rose from under the tree, and, taking eight steps to the north, he walked backwards and forwards eighteen paces to the east and to the west. If you will go outside the temple you will find a long low stonework about three feet high, upon which are still preserved nineteen stone lotuses, set there in primitive days to mark the spots at which flowers sprang up beneath the Master's feet. Going on a few yards further you will turn the corner of the temple to the left and stand beneath the Bò-tree. This is beyond question the lineal descendant of the tree beneath whose branches Buddha sat.* It grows eight feet from the centre of the western wall and its branches brush up against the stained plaster and brick of the plinth of the temple. Beneath it there is on the one side another old altar built up against the wall, and, on the other, actually

* In the Museum in Calcutta there are preserved several considerable fragments of the dead roots found *underneath* the original "Diamond Throne," roots which must be those of the sacred tree itself.

supporting one of its biggest boughs, is an old stone doorway buttressed by a casing of modern bricks. A low wall of plastered brick encloses on three sides a little area in which these relics stand, and outside this little enclosure again is a clear space, which runs also all round the temple, and was used for the frequent circumambulations necessary in the ritual of the Buddhist faith. This clear space is of especial holiness, and was once shut off by the stone railing which the Emperor Asoka set up about the year 240 B.C. The original temple built by Asoka was very different from that which we see to-day. As far as it can be reconstructed now, it seems to have consisted of a high wall enclosing a space, of which the greatest dimensions were from north to south. In the middle of this a pillared stone temple rose, and, in the centre of it, the "Diamond Throne," somewhat entangled with the branches of the Bò-tree towards the west. This, with the exception of the nineteen lotus foot-marks, is perhaps the only part of the temple that has remained in its exact original site from the earliest days to these. Most of the information which we possess as to the original shape of the shrine set up to protect this holy spot is derived from the carvings upon the railing at Bharhut. There is no question that these are intended to represent the shrine at Buddh-Gaya, and, crude as they are, they present adequate evidence of the original appearance of the temple.

But the real intention of this chapter is not so much to describe the archæological interests of Buddh-Gaya as to tell the story of the greatest pilgrim of all who ever made the journey and worshipped there. Only three white persons were present on the day on which the Tashi Lama made his formal obeisance before the spot on which, by the unswerving belief of Northern Buddhism, he himself, Buddha, and no other, had received enlightenment more than two thousand years ago. It is difficult for a Western European to put himself in a position wholly to understand the importance of this visit. Buddha, that is to say, that divine spirit which returned to earth in the person of the Great Teacher, is reincarnated in a greater or less degree in several of the great members of the Tibetan Hierarchy, but the Most Precious Teacher, His Holiness the Grand Lama of Tashi-lhunpo, is regarded by the Northern Buddhists not merely as the Vicegerent upon earth of the divinity, the only position that his nearest parallel, the Pope, may claim, but actually as the prolongation in this world of the spirit and essence of Buddha himself. That is to say, for the little crowd of red or yellow garmented men who sat beneath the Bò-tree at Buddh-Gaya on the twenty-second of December, 1905, the occasion was no less than that of Buddha himself revisiting the scene of his trial and his triumph, after its abandonment and desecration for many centuries. To this soul-stirring situation there can hardly be a parallel in Christianity or in Islam. I had the luck to be one of the three Englishmen who witnessed it.

About eleven o'clock, His Holiness, a quiet and refined-looking man, with one of the pleasantest smiles I have ever seen in my life, entered his state palanquin and was borne through the little village to the gate in the eastern wall of the sacred enclosure. The path from here to the main gate of the temple, which immediately faces it, is somewhat cumbered up with pillars and torii, and at that moment was still further littered with some of the posts of the Asokan railing, which the Mahant or his predecessors had taken away as building stone, and which have only just been restored. The palanquin was set down outside the temple door, and the Grand Lama stepped out of it. Moving steadily and with a natural grace, which comes

The Great Buddha on the Diamond Throne Buddh-Gaya.

[*Facing page* 250.

easily, perhaps, to one who has from his infancy received as a matter of unquestioned right the worship men pay to gods, he walked up over the rice and flower-strewn floor into the outer chamber and stood for a moment at the entrance of the inner shrine. The sight was one that it is impossible fully to describe. For the nonce the inner room, with its great Buddha seated upon the throne, had been transformed into a Tibetan sanctuary. Upon the Diamond Throne flared and smoked a hundred little butter-lamps of brass. Great katags swathed the shoulders of the idol, almost covering the permanent cloak and the official robes with which the Mahant had decked it for the day. (At the same time he had almost entirely destroyed its beauty by regilding and repainting the face: so far as he could help it, there was little left of the great peace which marks the countenance of Buddha from Mukden to Ceylon, and the mark of Vishnu had been repainted with malicious distinction upon the forehead.) On either side of the little chamber two rows of squatting monks muttered a monotone of prayer. A little to the right of the doorway the figure of the Crown Prince of Sikkim alternately raised itself to a kneeling position and then again resumed the motionless and prone attitude in which alone he dared contemplate the holiness of the place and of the occasion. On either side of the Grand Lama, as he paused for a moment at the threshold, was a Tibetan monk of high rank. One was the sagacious-looking face of His Holiness's prime minister; on the other side—and it was towards him that at this supreme moment of his life the Grand Lama leaned—was the friend of his childhood and of his manhood, his old and beloved tutor. The Lama himself was dressed with perfect taste, not in his golden robes of incarnate divinity, but in the plain dark crimson frock of a common monk. His lips moved automatically; and then he stepped forward, and, before taking his seat upon a cushion, he bowed once slowly and as an equal before the great image of Prince Gautama, letting his forehead sink down and touch the edge of the Diamond Throne. He then retired and assisted pontifically at the service which continued before, during and after his arrival without apparent reference to himself. The doorway and the outer chamber were thronged with jostling pilgrims. The larger part were, of course, Tibetans, who had come down in the suite of the Grand Lama, but there were representatives also from Burma, Ceylon, Siam, Nepal, and even Japan. The heavy coils of blue incense smoke mixed with the brown reek of the smoking butter-lamps and drifted out through the high doorways into the sunny spaces of the outer air. The drone of many smothered repetitions made a volume of incomprehensible sound, which was mastered now and again by the louder monotone, rising and falling again across the open door, of the Buddhist monks, who had from the earliest dawn been wandering round and round the temple, always in the same direction as the hands of a clock, clicking the beads of their rosaries and murmuring the everlasting anthem "Om mani péme hum."

An hour later the Grand Lama, dressed in his full splendour of gold silk brocade, came from inside the temple and took up his seat upon the outer throne to the west beneath the branches of the Bò-tree itself. Here the Buddhist mass was sung. Tibetans are very jealous of the presence of strangers at this particular service. I therefore had asked Captain O'Connor to sound the Grand Lama as to whether he would object to my making a sketch of the incident. Permission was at once and willingly given, and in the coloured plate which forms the frontispiece to this book there is at least this interest, that, whatever its artistic demerits, it represents one of the most absorbing incidents of religious history that have ever taken place. Even the most bigoted opponent of what a misinformed West calls idolatry will admit the unique situation in which, if the description will be pardoned by theoretic Buddhists, the god of a religion returns for the first time after many centuries to revisit the scene of his incarnation, his trial, and his victory. The leaves of the Bò-tree rustle lightly in the warm breeze, and little dots of sunlight filter down upon the gold and crimson of the kneeling monks. There is the distant cry of a child herding buffaloes back from the river to the village.

In an hour's time the mass was over. The water and the rice had been distributed and the last benediction said. Then came the ceremonial reception of the pious by the Grand Lama, and with the rest His Holiness received ourselves. There was the exchange of a katag, a moment's pressure of the hand and a kindly word or two in Tibetan, which, alas! only Captain O'Connor could understand. Chairs were given us on the Grand Lama's right hand, and we watched the ceremony and the varying salutations

Under the Bô-tree, Buddh-Gaya.

[*Facing page* 254.

accorded each pilgrim with much interest. The kindliest of all, an actual touching of the brow with his own, was given to the old tutor. Tea was then given us. Tibetan tea, as all the world knows, is mixed with butter and salt, and becomes rather a thin greasy soup than anything which is known to Europe. The Grand Lama (bless his kindly heart) had heard that we barbarians drank tea with sugar, and with the best of intentions he had prepared a special brew for us, in which, on the top of the salt and butter, he had added handfuls of sugar. Even O'Connor, who is more or less used to Tibetan drinks, quailed before this awful beverage. There was another kindly salutation, and the Grand Lama was borne back to his home, while the great majority of the monks resumed their circumambulations, muttering absently the while.

All day long it went on. There is no such holy place in all the universe as that which is surrounded by the rails of Buddh-Gaya, and the merit which a man may acquire by walking round and round is greater than that which he may lay up for himself anywhere else on earth. There is a sacred road at Lhasa, round which thousands of pilgrims annually move, within the loop of which even the infidel and the stranger may, in dying, reach to Nirvana. There is the even holier tract that surrounds the cathedral at Lhasa, and the present writer had once no inconsiderable chance of discovering by personal experience whether a mere Christian actually departing this life on that street would, or would not, go straight to Nirvana as Lamaism assures the world. But this is more sacred than either. Far into the night the hum of pilgrims' voices came up through the darkened trees, and by the red tossing light of a thousand high-flaring lamps ranged upon every crevice and sill of the exterior of the temple, one might still see the patient Buddhists celebrating this most holy opportunity by the performance of the circumambulation by repeated prostrations. This most effective act of worship entails the lying down of the pilgrim at full length upon the ground. He stretches out his arms and makes a slight mark in the dust. A prayer is then said, and the pilgrim rises and sets his feet upon the mark he has made. After another prayer he again stretches himself out full length upon the ground, making another mark with his outstretched fingers. This process is repeated until he has arrived at the place from which he started. It was a strange thing to go down among the scented flowers and occasional

BUDDHGAYA.

wafts of incense in the dark night to see the weird worship of these human "loopers" in the fitful light of the wasting illuminations, and it made a fitting termination to one of the most interesting days I have ever spent in my life.

South India.

THERE is something about Southern India in general which marks it off very distinctly from the India that is usually known to the touring visitor. Its remoteness from the great centres of Mohammedan religion, and, therefore, its freedom from the influences of Islam, its very luxuriant vegetation, and, therewith, of course, its warmer climate—all these have conspired to make the characteristics of the Deccan and the Carnatic very different from those which strike the eye so clearly in the north. Here is that India which is traditionally known to Western nations. Much that mediæval travellers have written about the India that they knew, is, in these days, true only of Travancore and Cochin. Here in the south there is no busy and commercial competition; here the chattering and seditious Bengalis never penetrate. It is a lotus-eating land, where superstition flourishes and caste binds down its votaries with an iron hand. Here the more

The old Dutch Fort, Quilon.

[*Facing page 258.*

venturesome traveller among the backwaters of the west, or a sportsman from Quilon, that green gem of tropical India, pursuing his quarry far into the ravines of the Ghats, will still find the simple life that was known to Vasco Da Gama and Sir Thomas Roe. Here he will find villages where human sacrifice has but recently been abolished. Stranger still, he will find out-caste tribes of Santals who will die of hunger rather than accept food from the hands of Brahmins! Still on the Nilgiris there await him the thatched huts with finials of stone where a dead girl is married to any chance passer-by in order that she may escape the awful punishment that awaits the spinster in the next world. Still he may find the ordeal by fire carried out, or, at least, some old resident who will tell him, truly enough, that he has seen with his own eye the Sanyasi walk confidently across the red-hot bars of iron. Nay, in Madras itself you will find at His Excellency's evening parties that the relative aristocracy of the native girls is in inverse ratio to the length of their skirts—in a word, you will still find nearly all that in your childhood made stories of India so fearsome and so fascinating.

If this is true of the ordinary life of the Carnatic, it is true in a very special manner of the great

South Indian temples. Up in the north of India the European, if the truth must be told, is little anxious to penetrate into, or stay long within, even the most famous of Hindoo or Sikh temples. Twenty minutes exhaust for some people the inside even of the Golden Temple at Amritsar, and though he is indignantly repelled from its namesake at Benares, no traveller really believes that inside that crowded-upon and insignificant building there is much to be seen of interest. It is far different in the south. Already, at Puri, one would give an ear to get inside, and once south of the Kistna, nothing proves so finally and irrefutably the gulf that exists between east and west as two or three hours spent in such a building as the Great Temple of Madura.

It is difficult to take one of these temples as being entirely typical of the rest. Each presents overpoweringly distinct features, though in certain respects there is no doubt a similarity of sentiment and architecture. The whole plan of these great and sacred shrines has been framed with a view to increase in every possible way the solemnity of the innermost sanctuary. At Srirangam there are no fewer than seven square enclosing walls, each of which contains between itself and the

The Main Gateway, Tanjore.

[*Facing page* 260.

next a human warren of temple servitors. The outer wall of this "nest" of concentric squares, if the phrase may be permitted, is 3,072 feet in length and 2,521 feet in width, 20 feet 8 inches in height and 6 feet wide at the top. Now it is difficult to appreciate the real meaning of these figures. They can perhaps best be understood by reference to a map of London. One side of the temple wall would reach from the statue of Wellington outside the Royal Exchange to beyond that of Queen Anne outside the west front of St. Paul's Cathedral, while the side at right angles from the Royal Exchange would just reach across the river to the southern approach to London Bridge. In area this one temple is thus equivalent to about one-fourth of the City.

Tanjore is magnificent; half-fort, half temple, it stands secure without the city. Hampi's huge pyramid-spire mourns yet the desolation among the ruins beneath the banyans of the river bank. Madura is a city in itself mysteriously pent up within its high red walls and heaven-piercing gates.

The regulations dealing with the exclusion from these temples of persons in inferior caste are very curious. Certain pariahs are not allowed even to approach the outermost portal. Other classes are allowed in proportion to their racial status to penetrate into the temple, passing underneath the great gopura-crowned gateways one after another. One by one the less worthy castes are left behind until there comes a moment when the Englishman himself is civilly told that he must no longer intrude.*

In South India, it will not be denied by anyone who has travelled through these centres of religious life

* This question of an Englishman's status remains, so long as we are the ruling caste in India, of little practical importance, but it is of interest from other points of view. In this particular case the Englishman appears to occupy a position immediately below the Brahmin caste; but it need hardly be said that this is merely a local convention for the purpose of showing courtesy to the white man and at the same time of safeguarding the privacy of the shrine itself. Elsewhere in India the white man is outside caste. He is not above it, because, as has happened to the writer himself in Benares, his shadow passing over a tray of chains of marigolds will so far defile them that they may no longer be sold for presentation in the temple. Most emphatically he is not below it. The position of the Englishman is fairly well recognized, and it is illustrated by a curious story connected with the Durbar. The position of the Maharana of Udaipur has already been referred to as something quite outside all ordinary precedents. At the time of the Durbar of 1903 the very thorny question arose as to the relative rank, or rather rights, of a man like him, to whose social superiority all India as one man assents, and that of the Mohammedan Nizam of Hyderabad, who holds chief place among the native chiefs by right of a definite treaty concluded with his predecessors. The Maharana was approached by his Resident, who pointed out to him that we could not take sides in the religious disputes of India, but must obey the terms of the treaty which we had sworn to keep. The Maharana was in a difficult position. He fully saw the justice of our claim, but from his point of view it was impossible for him in the slightest degree to relax the everlasting claims of his race and faith. He made a curious suggestion. "If," said he, "the Government of India will place between the Nizam and myself any white man of whatsoever degree, I will sit in Durbar with the Nizam." This estimate of the Englishman as a kind of non-conductor is perhaps as suggestive of the real position occupied by ourselves in India as could well be made. It is, at the same time, a curious fact that this same Maharana of Udaipur in his own palace preserves so strictly the traditions of his race that his wife, the Maharani, is not allowed to see, or to be seen even by princesses of the Imperial English House.

BUDDHIST CAVE, ELLORA

that few influences in India possess the fascination of one of these majestic memorials of human labour and human devotion. Perhaps the temple at Madura is more impressive than others. Once within the great thirty-foot wall of red stone, which shuts in the temple on all sides, the visitor is allowed to wander at will through a labyrinth of dark halls and passages and columned chambers. The forbidden precincts here are of small extent, and he must be an unimaginative man indeed who can pass through the cloisters without a touch of awe.

Outside, the strong white glare of the Indian noon beats down mercilessly upon the infinite carvings of the gopura. Strange beasts writhe and quarrel in red sandstone among the tangled yet orderly ornaments of the tapering pyramid—bosses, cartouches, panels, knops, billet-mouldings, courses of egg and lotus pattern, flame-like edgings that follow faithfully round the deep-cut ascending lines, or fail for a moment where a fluted plaque stands boldly out amid the complicated symmetry of its own wide course. For each course is repeated by that above it in a lessening scale, until the design changes at the very summit of the gopura. Here a ridge supports eight or nine gilded finials, while at the end, on either side of the great wedge of red stone, a fine shell-like ornament over-arches the symbol of the divinity there honoured. The play of light and shade upon a gopura is infinite. Never does it take on the same appearance from sunrise to sunset. Infinite variety is caused by the shadows of its deep-cut ornaments changing from minute to minute, and the very hues of the warm apricot stone, visited or abandoned by the sun from hour to hour, change as the lights and colours of distant peaks.

Inside, there is a gloom of white pillars and a whispering of bats like the shaking together of a bunch of thin steel ribbons. Only after reflection back and forth does a meagre light bear in from some unaccountable shaft, and by it you may dimly observe the dark corridor in which you walk, supported on either side by great grotesquely carved piers and ceiled above with twenty-foot slabs of stone. In just as uncertain a mystery of light and shade we pass through to the labyrinth of pillars in a side shrine half an acre in extent, where, thrust forward so that no chance of missing them may occur, figures and groups obscene and foul intrude themselves to ward off that curious superstition of all South India—the baleful influences of an Englishman's evil eye.

A sanctuary in Madura.

[Facing page 264.

The natives pay one little attention. If they resent one's presence, which is doubtful, they do not show it, while the superior officials of the temple are wise enough to know that the travelling Englishman generally leaves behind him in one way or another very substantial bakshish. As likely as not, while you are looking at some curious figure of a dancing goddess, or a prancing yali, you will find your shoulder gently rubbed, and a second afterwards the great mass of an elephant's trunk will slide down over your shoulder begging for money with its nervous little finger-like projection as eloquently as any one of the children in the town outside. Most of us know how difficult and tiresome a job it is to pick up a sixpence from a hard surface just after the nails have been cut, and there is something positively miraculous in the dexterity with which an elephant with his apparently clumsy trunk will raise from the stone floor even the smallest of Indian coins.

It was a Tamil who first used the famous expression, now paraphrased in almost every country, that "an arch never sleeps." Whether this be true or not, it is clear from all experience that an arch can be drugged into stability for a period of years long enough in all conscience for any human structure. Few persons in Egypt ever come away without a genuine regret that the master builders of olden times were either unacquainted with, or, if they knew of it, deliberately neglected, this principle. It is difficult to set bounds to the possibilities of architecture unfettered by modesty, expense, or the lack of labour, if a man like Khufu or Rameses XII. had but had his ideas of magnificence whetted by a knowledge of the arch. In the same way the vast amount of labour expended on even such a temple as Srirangam fails a little to produce the result desired because of the necessarily short views that always have to be taken in buildings which depend for the width of their aisles upon the longest possible beam that can be safely hewn from the local variety of stone. Men like Tirumala Nayakka realised this want of lightness and endeavoured to supply it by supporting the ceilings of their choultris upon hundreds of slender and delicately carved columns. Some of the most beautiful effects of these South Indian temples are gained in this way. The thousand gradations of grey light that penetrate into these avenues of stone, deflected, reflected, obstructed, cut off, ever dwindling in intensity as the centre of the hall is reached, make a tangled chiaroscuro of light and

The Processional Car, Seringapatam.

In a South Indian Temple.

[*Facing page* 266.

shade such as I think is rarely seen elsewhere. But on the other hand there is, in these close forests of stone, a haunting sense of oppression from which one is never wholly free.

This is the more remarkable because, in other parts of Southern India, the rock-cut temples not only exhibit a sound appreciation of wide internal vistas, but seem, especially in the case of the chief Buddhist case at Ellora, to have understood not merely the principle of the arch, but the timbering necessary to support a roof-vault. This temple at Ellora, of which a photograph is here annexed, is one of the wonders of India. It dates from about the third century of the Christian era, and, as a title of honour, is called the Cave of Visvakarma, the same divine carpenter whose work we have already seen at Mandalay and Puri. It seems almost impossible that architects who here used needlessly and for sheer ornament a Gothic arched roof and apse should have been totally ignorant of what they so nearly expressed.

There is a wave of Buddhism beginning again to make itself felt in India after twelve centuries, and the proposal has been made that these Buddhist caves shall be handed over to trustees on behalf of the many thousand Buddhist pilgrims who annually visit their sacred and historic places in India.

At Ellora there is also, of course, the Kailas, a Hindu temple of a much later day, which appeals so strongly to the sense of picturesqueness possessed by travellers that the Buddhist caves are comparatively little known. In truth, there is some excuse for the neglect. The whole building is carved out of the living rock of the hillside, outside as well as in, and covered with carvings, isolated statues, or groups. Every string course is as faithfully represented as if it followed its due level of masonry, and only a certain weather-worn discontinuity in the face of the temple wall betrays the fact that it has not been built in the usual way. It stands in a roughly-squared area round which rise precipices of rock culminating in a little flash of vivid green where the hill-side vegetation hangs a bouquet into the pit, and each wall is honeycombed at its base with strange galleries and pillared ante-chambers even more strangely decorated. Stone elephants stand in eternal attendance. A gate-pierced barrier, as well finished as the temple, hides it from the outside, where, a hundred feet lower, the long flat Indian plain stretches out interminably—flat, hot, and adequately tilled.

RAMESWARAM

Of all the Southern Indian temples, Rameswaram is best worth a visit. It lies on an island between India and Ceylon, famous in old days for having been a pier of the bridge across which Rama pursued Ravana, King of Ceylon, and brought Sita back again, now chiefly receiving attention because it must be a pier of a very different bridge—that which will join up the railway systems of Ceylon and India.

One joggles across from Mandapam in a little steamer in company with a mixed collection of pilgrims—Rameswaram ranks third in holiness, after Benares and Puri—steering apparently to all points of the compass at random, but really following the one tortuous channel deep enough for the five-foot draught of our little ferry. Once landed at Pamban, a Pilgrim's Way takes us for eight miles east to Rameswaram. It is a pretty road. It is not a good road. Indeed, it is in some ways as bad a road as exists anywhere upon the flat, but it is very beautiful. The straight-running track keeps between kerbstones which in most places have sunk into the overgrown roadside edges. Overhead there is an almost continuous green canopy of trees, either hemmed in at their roots by tangled undergrowth, or spaced largely by emerald grass plots. Rest houses of quaint carved stone await the weary pilgrims who are to be seen going and coming continually wrapped in meditation, and thumb-nailing off the beads of some rosary of crimson-dyed kernels.

Rameswaram is reached on the edge of the water, and the sand whirled up by the south-westerly monsoon has sadly chafed its seaward wall. Inside there are the vast corridors for which the temple is famed, a full-throated bazaar in the main aisle, more corridors, bathing tanks, more corridors still, and then the forbidden central shrine. I dare say there is not very much going on in these sacred enclosures. Elsewhere is a photograph taken, more by luck than management, of the inner court at Srirangam, whereto access is denied to all but Brahmins ; probably Rameswaram's central shrine is as uninspiring. But until some Brahmin is born with the gifts needed to-day for scientific research, and the willingness to use them, we shall never know very much of what goes on in these innermost sanctuaries.

Here, on the sands beside the sea at the last outpost of India, the journey ends. One of these days I will piece together another mosaic of Indian towns ; to my mind there will not be less of interest because the places will be less known than those which for the most part have given their names to the chapters in this book. But, for the present, an end has to be made somewhere, and here let it be, beside the south-eastward reaching sand-banks, hot in the sun, up which the little tides of Palk Strait ripple transparently. Behind us is a monotonous drum-beating, surmounting the long grey wall of the temple, and overhead is the crisp rustling of hard palm fronds one against another in the light air. It is the last rood of India, and over there you can see the dark line of cocoanuts which means Ceylon.

The Later Days of Nana Sahib.

NANA SAHIB was driven out of Cawnpore by Havelock on the 16th of July, 1857. He retired through Bithur, where, amid the busy preparations and precautions which his defeat had rendered necessary, he found time to order the slaughter of Mrs. Carter and her month-old infant, the only European left within his reach. It is to the lasting credit of the widow of Baji Rao, and of Kasi Bai, Nana's youngest wife, that they had, six weeks before, protected Mrs. Carter, vowing that they would destroy themselves if a woman in her condition were killed. Now, however, they found themselves powerless. Nana's savage determination grew with every check he received. Bala Rao his younger brother weakened in adversity, but was swept along by the new energy of the rebel leader, who, realising that the English were barely strong enough to hold Cawnpore itself, returned, and, taking up his residence again at Bithur, actively superintended the revolt in the North-West Provinces. His greatest hope lay in the reinforcements from Gwalior under Tantia Topi. The latter seems to have been a loyal servant, but took no pains to conceal his contempt for the capacity and pluck of Nana's generals, none of whom were given posts of responsibility in the force of about twenty-five thousand well-armed men, who now drew in to Bithur, and awaited the command to recapture Cawnpore.

The last occasion on which Nana Sahib is certainly known to have been in the field against us was on the 6th of December, 1857. Cawnpore, during the temporary absence of Sir Colin Campbell, had been retaken by the rebels, and Tantia Topi offered battle from a well-chosen position. Sir Colin, however, drove him headlong, and the pursuit of the main body was continued for fourteen miles along the Kalpi road. Nana Sahib, however, wheeled off to the north-west, along the Grand Trunk road, and, halting at Bithur only long enough to pick up his family and servants, was able to distance the pursuit of General Hope Grant, who was delayed by the need of securing the guns abandoned by Nana's flying rabble at Serai Ghat, twenty-five miles from Cawnpore. Major Russell was sent on with a small force, but, after a stern chase across Oude, he failed to overtake the fugitives, who just made good their escape across the Nepal frontier.

So much is known. What happened afterwards to Nana Sahib has hitherto been the merest conjecture. It was, however, reported that the notorious rebel died in the following year of malarial fever, contracted in the jungles of the "terai." As can be imagined, Lord Canning's government were not anxious to disprove the rumour. Nana's continued existence would have been the source of never-ending disquiet. He would have been, till his death, a centre round which disaffection must naturally rally, and entirely as Sir Jang Bahadur was trusted, it was felt by everyone that Nana's death was by far the best solution of the difficulty. In the absence of definite information, the reward of fifty thousand rupees, which was placed upon his head, was not cancelled, but to the relief of everyone the report of his death at this date came to be generally credited, and was eventually accepted by Indian historians. It is true, however, that from time to time a little uncertainty was felt, and the issue of *The Times* of December 28th, 1860, contained a letter definitely stating that Nana Sahib was still alive and in Tibet, and that the rumour of his death in 1858 had been deliberately circulated for political reasons. It was also said that in 1859 one of Hope Grant's men actually offered to bring him into the camp. But years passed, no corroboration or further news was published, and the original story came to be accepted by all, though, in the absence of definite information, from time to time a rumour spread itself that Nana had once again been discovered as an old man in one part of India or another. It will hardly be believed, but even in January of this present year, 1906, a report was circulated that the aged criminal had again been found. Luckily perhaps for Nana, there was something to substantiate the report of his death in 1858, and the search for him slackened in consequence. But it was Bala Rao, his brother, who actually died in that year.

Before going on, it is necessary to re-state some of the facts connected with Nana Sahib's position. Many people to-day may be ignorant of the reasons which induced the rebels of 1857 to accept the guidance of Nana, and even those who are well acquainted with the facts may be glad of something to remind them of the details of the Peshwa's pedigree.

Nana Sahib's name was Dhandu Pant. He was the second son of Madho Rao Bhao Bhat, whose wife was the sister of the wife of Baji

Rao, the last Peshwa of Poona. Baji Rao was the representative of the Mahratta claim to the Empire of India, and when he went into compulsory retirement, there is no doubt that he took with him the sympathy of a large number of Hindus, though his personal record was not of the best. The English government treated him with generosity. It allowed him the handsome pension of £80,000 a year—he was childless, and it was made clear from the outset that this was to be a personal annuity, and would not descend to anyone—and permission to choose his own place of residence. He chose Bithur, a town about thirteen miles north-north-west of Cawnpore.

It is, of course, necessary for a Hindu to have a son—by blood or adoption—to perform necessary funeral rites, and for that reason Baji Rao, in his childlessness, cast about for a boy whom he might adopt. His choice fell upon Dhandu Pant, together with another who died soon afterwards and whose place was filled ultimately by Gangadhai Bhat or Bala Rao, Dhandu Pant's younger brother, a man of no character.

Dhandu Pant was chosen because, by Hindu law—and the Bhats, though the name seems vulgar, were, by blood, Konkanasta Brahmins of the straitest sect—an eldest son may not be adopted. His eldest brother, Baba Bhat, was thus passed over and always appears in the history of the Mutiny as his younger brother's subordinate. He escaped detection in 1858, and, it is said, actually lived for many years in the Sanjaoli bazaar near Simla, disguised as an ascetic. He acted as Nana's treasurer and was High Commissioner of Cawnpore at the time of the Massacre. Dhandu adopted the name by which he is universally known, Nana Sahib, and went to live with Baji Rao at Bithur.

The ex-Peshwa's choice of Bithur—or, as it was then frequently called, Brahma-wat—as the place of his exile, is significant. Although the Company's Intelligence Department seem to have forgotten the fact, Bithur is well known to Hindus as the especial place of resort of those who have a grievance. It is reputed to be the accomplisher of every injured man's object. Immediately after the transference of Baji Rao to this auspicious spot, Brahmins from Benares, and from the south, flocked hither, and mystic rites were performed —rites, however, which did not prevent Baji Rao dying in 1851 without seeing any fruit thereof. Meanwhile Nana Sahib showed no unwillingness to make friends with the English; he even went out of his way to invite parties of officers and ladies to Bithur.

But the seeds of trouble were sown in 1851, when Nana Sahib—to take the most trustworthy evidence—was twenty-seven years old. Baji Rao, in his will, left property to Nana which has been estimated at two million pounds. But Nana immediately claimed in addition the continuance to himself of Baji Rao's huge pension. This was refused. The Court of Directors, as an act of grace, offered him the revenues of a small district, but this olive-branch was rejected, and Azimullah Khan was despatched to London to plead his cause. This attempt was unsuccessful, but Nana, biding his time, showed little resentment, and remained on excellent terms with the garrison of Cawnpore.

It is not necessary to tell again the only too well-known story of Cawnpore. When Nana fled north to Nepal, he took with him the widow of the late Peshwa and his own wife, Kasi Bai. This girl—for even then she was not fourteen years old—was the daughter of one Ramchandra Sakharam Karmakar. She had been married for some years previously, but sent to Nana only in 1854, when she was ten. Her name was originally Sundra Bai, and she was known in Nana's household both as Kasi Bai and Krishna Bai. She was also frequently called Kaku Bai. This confusion of names is characteristic of everyone concerned. Most of the Nana's adherents had two names, and many even more. Kasi Bai and her adoptive mother-in-law, as has been said, had attempted to save Mrs. Carter's life. When, on the 6th of December, they were taken with Nana on his flight, they took with them two ladies, natives of Brahma-wat, who were living, and long afterwards lived, under Kasi Bai's protection, though their relations with Nana admitted of no doubt. With them also went Bala Rao, his brother, Tantia Topi the younger, Baba Godbole, Jannu Singh, and Parusram Jagmal, old servants of Nana's. It is probable that Tantia Topi the elder and his wife accompanied Nana on this occasion, but, if so, he must almost immediately have left Nana and made his way back to India.

The story of their reception over the frontier is strange. They were received by Kedarnath Singh, a Nepalese general, who had been specially deputed to meet them by Sir Jang Bahadur, the Prime Minister. He escorted them to a small village called Deondari, probably identical with the Deongarh of the map, near Tribeni Ghat. There they awaited orders. It must have been an anxious moment for Nana. Neutrality is a product of the west, and the fugitives may well have encountered on the road some of the contingent of eight thousand that Nepal was sending to the help of the English at that time. Moreover, Jang Bahadur had an ugly method of dealing with emergencies. But there was no help for it. There was no safety for Nana in India, as he knew well enough. At last Jang Bahadur arrived in person. His terms were simple. Kasi Bai and the other women and the servants were to put themselves under the protection of the Prime Minister. Nana was apparently offered no asylum, but a hint may have been conveyed to him that Jang Bahadur would wink at his escape in disguise. It seems certain that Nana never saw his own people again, even in Nepal, except in this stealthy way. The terms were agreed to. Nana and Tantia handed over their wives and offered to go westwards in the robe of Atits.* The dress was provided and the exchange made.

At the last moment one final arrangement had to be made. Drawing from his pocket the famous "Nau-lakha," the principal jewel of the Peshwas, he offered to sell it to Jang Bahadur. It is—for it exists still—a long necklace of pearls, diamonds, and emeralds, and is perhaps without a rival in the world. It is estimated to-day—some small additions have been made to it—to be worth one hundred thousand pounds. The unsympathetic Prime Minister saw his chance. Instead of the nine hundred thousand rupees, which its very

* Atits are mendicants of the Saivite sect. They claim entertainment, and on the "angels unawares" principle generally obtain it.

name proclaimed to be its real value, he offered ninety-three thousand—£9,300—and Nana, compelled to take the offer or leave it, accepted the money. Here, however, Kasi Bai interposed. She would prefer, she said, not to come to Khatmandu and receive the price in hard cash. Would Jang Bahadur give her a village or two instead? So the Prime Minister, conscious perhaps of having driven a hard bargain with the helpless, agreed, in return for the necklace, to farm out to her the revenues of Dhangara and Raharia for four thousand five hundred rupees a year, which gave her a margin of between six and seven thousand rupees a year, besides the four hundred a month which Jang Bahadur allowed her for her maintenance. Thus the shrewd little lady secured a return of nearly eight per cent. upon the price of the necklace.*

Then, the two men† in their "girna-basta" dress took each a small "danda" in his hand, and went out to the west, and as he turned away

* The Maharaja of Darbhanga owns this necklace now. It descended through Ranodip Singh, Jang Bahadur's son, to Maharaja Bir Shamsher, whose widow sold it for its full value, 900,000 rupees, to the Maharaja Deb Shamsher, then Prime Minister. He was expelled, and, carrying the jewels with him, sold them at twenty-four hours' notice to the present Maharaja of Darbhanga. Accustomed as Calcutta is to displays of gems, the sight of this necklace upon the Maharaja on the occasion this year of laying the foundation-stone of the Victoria Memorial Hall caused something of a stir, though its history was probably known to few.

† As is well known, Tantia Topi was eventually caught and hanged at Sipri in 1859.

Nana Sahib said, "I cannot live in the hills or in the terai. I will go to the west, to some country where these sahibs are not in power." So Kasi Bai and her small court were left, and they went far to the extreme east of Nepal, to Dhangara, a village on the Kosi, not far from the Bengal frontier. But before she left the neighbourhood of Deondari, Bala Rao, Nana's brother, sickened and died of malarial fever. This was in many ways a good thing for everyone, for it started the report of Nana's own death, and things were kept so secret that General Sidhiman Singh, governor of the western terai, once assured an English officer that he had been present at Nana Sahib's burning in the Bhutwal district near Deongarh.

Life at Dhangara was not as uneventful for Kasi Bai as might have been expected. It may as well be confessed at once that she was far from being faithful to Nana. Jang Bahadur she could perhaps hardly resist, but the list of her lovers is much more extensive. Young Tantia Topi was probably the favoured one, but it seems that there was also some justification for the jealous feud between Narazon Rao—a servant of Nana's who was once arrested in India as Nana himself; his other name was Nana Safiri—and Bulwant Rao, who was, by the way, young Tantia Topi's half-brother. Accusation and counter-accusation eventually resulted in the expulsion of Narazon Rao and the imprisonment of Bulwant Rao.

In the latter case, the actual ground of the accusation was that Bulwant Rao had stolen jewels which Nana Sahib had entrusted to him to sell. As a matter of fact, Bulwant Rao behaved perfectly honestly. These jewels, to the value of 136,000 rupees, were sold in Lahore. Jang Bahadur, however, seized the opportunity of getting rid of a rival and Bulwant Rao remained for some time in prison. In this connection there was one of the strangest incidents of the whole story of Nana Sahib. Kasi Bai, who seems throughout to have been a good-hearted woman, actually approached the late Duke of Edinburgh during his tour in Nepal with a request that he should ask for Bulwant Rao's release. What a strange picture it is!

Three or four years after her arrival Kasi Bai sent a letter to her father in India, asking him to come and see her. With Oriental deliberation, he does so in 1866, and with him goes Azimullah Khan, Nana's late secretary. Now, in 1866, the belief that the famous rebel was dead had become universal, so that the worthy Sakharam was a little upset to notice that his daughter was still wearing the "tika," or spot of red turmeric, on the forehead, bangles on her wrists, and the kajur (antimony) adornment in her eyes. No Konkanasta widow could wear these proofs of "coverture" for a moment. Baji Rao's widow, who was living in the same house, had, of course, abjured them all. Azimullah Khan,* on his return to India, also assured one Ganesh, a chowkidar at Cawnpore, that Nana was still alive, and living under the protection of Sir Jang Bahadur. Indeed, in Nepal there seems to have been little concealment of the fact. Servants still watched over Nana's bed, "puja" was still made to Nana's silver chair and tulsi-leaves strewn before it. Nor was this all. The nightly talk in the kacheri of the "Begam's" house at Dhangara was of the coming of the Russians, and the reinstatement of Nana upon the throne.

One name occurs once or twice at this time. The residence of Nana is said to be a village called Thapa Téli. Thapa, or Thapu, seems to be a Nepalese word for a district or a village, but Téli is still unidentified. The only indication of its whereabouts is that Ririthang, which is apparently near to it, is said to be thirty-five days' march westwards of Dhangara. If the extreme difficulty of travelling in Nepal is not borne in mind, it might be thought almost impossible to spend thirty-five days in moving from one part of it to another. As it is,

* This man is believed afterwards to have made the pilgrimage to Mecca and died there.

it is probably an adequate description of the distance from Dhangara to Ririkot—"thang" means a plain and therefore probably applies to some portion of the district—which lies in the far west on the main road a few miles short of Sil Garhi. Thirty miles west again is a hamlet called Tila-téli, which may be the place referred to, especially if the adjacent mountains are known as the Dongsalian range. Wherever it is, Jang Bahadur seems to have allowed Nana Sahib to settle there under the pretence of keeping a shop, and to have settled a small monthly allowance of a hundred or hundred and fifty rupees upon the unhappy man. But every year about the time of the Shurat Mela, which took place in January or February, Nana, in the disguise of an Atit, returned to Dhangara. On these occasions, Kasi Bai, in the teeth of all Brahminical customs, superintended personally the distribution of food to pilgrims, and no doubt managed to snatch a few minutes' conversation with her husband.

In 1864 there had been a rumour among our troops at Diwangiri on the Assam frontier that Nana was present with the Tongsa Penlop and the Bhutanese army. In 1870, a near relative of the Governor of Bhutwal—where Nana is said to have died—testified from personal knowledge that he was still alive. Early in 1875 the definite news was received that he was then thirty-five days west of Trebeni Ghat (probably a slip), and an assurance was given that on March 5th he would come to make his annual visit to the Rani through Chitwan, "below Chandagiri." As a matter of fact, there seems to have been some delay, as the Atit mendicants did not arrive at Dhangara in that year till the latter days of April. There they received clothing and other presents, and started again westwards, a matter which was specially arranged by the Rani. Bulwant Rao seems to have been the accredited agent of Nana in these journeyings, and it is due to his activity that the Indian government received no more accurate information as to Nana's movements.

One more extraordinary piece of evidence remains. Nana Sahib, doubtless in his disguise as an Atit, from time to time attended the Kumbh Mela at Allahabad. It is almost inconceivable that he should thus put his head into the noose, but he must have been a desperate man, not unwilling perhaps to be caught, and once again, at any cost, to become the centre of any Indian disaffection. If one version of his latter days be true, at the close of his life Nana gave up all attempt at concealment. Be that as it may, no less a witness than the President of the Cow Protection Society has stated that so late as 1885 Nana Sahib dined with him on that festival.

Here we leave the hard road of ascertainable fact, and there is a choice of paths. One story, which was told to me by a well-known Rajput three or four years ago, is as definite as could be wished. It is to the effect that Nana, when between sixty and seventy years of age, was somewhat barbarously murdered in the terai by a man named Pulia Pamé, whose sister he had seduced some years before. The other story is very different and far more tragic. In 1895, at a place about thirty miles from Rajkot, an aged mendicant, who had been creating a disturbance in the road, was arrested. He said that he was Nana Sahib and claimed the protection of Sir Jang Bahadur, who had, of course, died many years before. The man was partially insane, and only excited merriment among his own countrymen. But he talked in his sleep of Nepal, and claimed that if he had his rights he would be Peshwa. Witnesses were collected, his bodily marks noted—apparently they bore out his contention to some extent*—and the

* In appearance Nana is said to have been rather above middle height, with a round face, and eyes peculiarly set. He was marked with small-pox, and some authorities say that he had a scar on his forehead. As to less visible characteristics, he may or may not have borne traces of an operation for varicocele. The man detained in 1895 seemed to some extent to correspond, and had in addition a scar on the back, evidently caused by a lanced carbuncle. Some day a chance medical diary, hitherto undiscovered, may decide the matter. The portrait of Nana Sahib, published in *The Illustrated London News* at the time of the Mutiny, is said to be quite unlike him.

Indian Government was consulted. Unutterably wise, Calcutta ordered that the witnesses should be dispersed and the man set free.

If there was any truth in the story, there is hardly a more desolate picture in history than that of Nana Sahib—old, discredited, half-witted, but still claiming the horrible honour of being himself, contemptuously set free by those whom he had so foully injured to wander still along the roads, the laughing-stock of his own people, vociferating his claims to idle wayfarers who soon passed on to their own business with a smile for the homeless and broken old man whose brains God had filled with illusion.

This is, perhaps, all we shall ever know of the later days of Nana Sahib.

Printed by The Chapel River Press, Kingston, Surrey.